KNOW ME, LIKE ME, FOLLOW ME

WHAT ONLINE SOCIAL NETWORKING MEANS FOR YOU AND YOUR BUSINESS

Penny Power

with Thomas Power

headline
business plus

First published in 2010 by
HEADLINE PUBLISHING GROUP

1

Cataloguing in Publication Data is available from the British Library

ISBN 978 07553 1951 0

Typeset in Caslon 540 by Avon DataSet Ltd,
Bidford-on-Avon, Warwickshire

Printed and bound in Great Britain by
Clays Ltd, St Ives plc

HEADLINE PUBLISHING GROUP
An Hachette UK Company
338 Euston Road
London NW1 3BH

www.headline.co.uk
www.hachette.co.uk

Dedication

This book is dedicated to Susan Kingham, an inspirational lady with the most extraordinary spirit. Her strength of love, empowerment and a belief in our family will live in us all forever.

ACKNOWLEDGEMENTS

This book has been twelve years in the making, although it took considerably less time to write it down. My journey into social networking started when Glenn Watkins, Thomas Power and I created Ecademy.

I would like to thank the following people for their incredible support and for the time they gave me so that through this book I could share so much of the richness of this new world:

Firstly, Thomas, my husband and business partner, without whose amazing awareness of this new world, his dedication to sharing new ideals and new tools, I would not have learned all that I have and been able to share them with you. He is truly awesome.

Creating Ecademy and learning how to live a twenty-first-century life as a businesswoman and as a parent is all thanks to our CEO Glenn Watkins, our favourite man in the world. Thank you, Glenn. You have developed a business that was impossible to see beyond a feeling and provided security and leverage for thousands of people around the world.

Thomas and I have learned so much about modern life. Most of our learning is thanks to our children who push us forward, support our dreams and have made our dreams 'family dreams'. Thank you, Hannah, Ross and TJ. You are amazing people and we never stop learning from you.

Thank you to one amazing unsung hero, Julian Bond, our CTO, who made Ecademy's site what it is today. He joined us in 2002 and brought new life into it and continues to interpret our ideas and turn them into code at remarkable speed.

Thanka to Sophia Watkins, Glenn's wife, for her unbelievable strength and commitment to Ecademy. Also Glenn and Sophia's two children, Alex and Libby.

I must thank the Ecademy members who have trusted and believed, been patient and been loving. You are the heartbeat that makes everything worthwhile. You continue to teach us and we continue to learn. I have the utmost respect for the way you live your lives through helping others and building personal brands that inspire and reflect the world we all want to be part of.

Thank you to John Moseley for seeing the need for this philosophy to be shared and coaching me through the process of writing. I will always remember you called me Mrs Comma! Thank you to Grant Leboff for suggesting I wrote a book and for introducing me to John. This all started with you, Grant.

Also to the following people who allowed me to interview them and have taught me great lessons along the way and form a tremendous part of this book:

William Buist, Ivan Misner, David Smith, Julie Meyer, Sue Richardson, Nigel Adams, Abha Banerjee, Claire Richmond, Nigel Biggs, Doug Holman, Jane Swift, Grant Leboff, Graham Jones, Nicole Wehden, Lizzi Vandorpe, Chuck Zdrojowy, Dave Clarke, Aron Stevenson, Roger

Knight, Roger Hamilton, James McBrearty, Duff Ross, Nigel Risner, Bjørn Guldager, James Knight, Philip Calvert, Michael Pokoky, Andreja Lajh, Leon Benjamin, Steve Clarke, Hannah Power, Louis Gray, Mark Sinclair, Linda Lloyd, Sally Church, Nick Tadd, Dirk Singer, Parke Ladd, Mark Earls and Kate Power.

This book has been created to share the knowledge of all these people and for all that they have given to that intention. I thank every one of you for this.

Please visit my blog www.knowmelikemefollowme.com to link to these contributors.

CONTENTS

INTRODUCTION

W E ARE ENTERING a period of humanity that is increasingly
based on social interaction. A world where having fun and
getting along with others is becoming a critical part of our
lives. In parallel with this is the importance of maintaining our
economic existence in a world that is suffering economic
downturn and where there is massive competition.

As we look at any media, be it TV, radio, newspapers or the
internet, we see that global leaders are looking for ways to
collaborate and ensure that as individuals we can survive the
financial problems that every economy across the world is
facing. But is it the responsibility of our governments to find
the solutions for us as individuals? We rely on them to provide
safety, education, health and governance but should we rely
on them, or anybody for that matter, to ensure that we thrive
emotionally and financially?

The advent of social networking and social media have
been the biggest boost for individuals to take responsibility
for their personal brand and build a strong financial future for
themselves. Every one of us holds the key to provide for

ourselves based on the experience, knowledge and expertise that we have. Being self-reliant and taking responsibility for our future is now a critical part of who we are.

It is becoming increasingly hard for companies to provide long-term security to individuals. The cost of running large businesses and the risks associated with permanent employment are only going to become greater. The one variable is the people and we know that people are expendable to companies. Individually we have to become suppliers.

Currently it is reported that 1.1 million people in the UK alone are believed to have second jobs – 662,000 of whom are women.[1] This is a fantastic development as the change is occurring at the same time as the growth in online social networking. Called social networks and social media for a reason, these places are helping people communicate, share knowledge and build businesses with the underlying aspect of being 'social'.

Social networks are enabling people to become brands in their own right and to build a reputation that people trust, like and want to follow. Being known, being liked and being followed as an expert is helping millions of people around the world build a secure future.

The knowledge economy is becoming a reality for everyone, from the homeopath through to the independent business consultant. Opportunities are being shared and businesses are being created because of the knowledge that people are willing to share online.

Social networks connect people. Facebook has successfully created a social engine that connects friends across the world. Now social networking is becoming commonplace in business – connecting people through knowledge. Knowledge has become your greatest asset. Once you know how to demonstrate and share it you can become a respected expert and build your own financial future.

While writing this book I utilized ten major networks online. The people I interviewed within these networks have changed their lives due to this new connected online world. The rise of the individual is what this century will be known for and this is the opportunity each of us must take to ensure that we no longer place our future in the hands of others. Taking personal responsibility for your life will define you as an individual and open up a world that you can enjoy being part of.

CHAPTER 1

THE WORLD IS REBOOTING

THE FACT THAT I have been asked to write a book is a small piece in the jigsaw of why I am qualified to teach you about 'a new way of doing business'. This alone will not give you the confidence to absorb my philosophies and advice. However, what I have done in my life will give you a picture of me and why I am able to share my thoughts with a level of expertise and experience.

The twenty-first century – what does this actually mean to you and to the business world you are part of? Are attitudes, behaviours and philosophies changing? If they are, what is the evidence and how will this impact those around you and those you care for? Can you feed your family in the future? These are the thoughts that drive me. There is no doubt that the social media sites are creating a change. Adapting to this new world is a challenge, but something that no one can ignore.

What is known and felt by everyone is that the world is fast paced, there is no margin for error. High expectations are the norm and the accelerating rate of change and problem-solving is phenomenal. Time is our most precious commodity and yet so many people still use their time unwisely, ineffectively and driven by habits of the past. We spend too little time thinking about how we need to adapt and not taking the risk to discover and become modern-day pioneers in our own right. Darwin noted that only the most adaptable will survive; this is truer now than at any time previously.

What I know is that everyone will be a supplier. Large organizations will not be able to offer jobs in the way they have in the past. The employment market is changing. Flexible working is not just a challenge for companies, it is also your challenge. Can you be sure that you will remain employed? The only way to survive is to create a brand that puts you in the front of the mind of anyone looking for your expertise. This sounds very dramatic, but look at the facts. Mass unemployment is all around us. Every day on the news another successful company is laying off staff. The implications of this are far and wide, both politically and economically. What I am focusing on is how to best equip yourself for this new world.

I remember going to America on holiday with my parents when I was fifteen. It was a fantastic experience. The most significant aspect of this experience was the level of customer service in the shops. The cheerful, helpful manner that was definitely not evident in the UK in the 1970s. I learned that staff in the USA were, on the whole, paid through commission – their income was related to the experience they gave everyone they met. I liked that.

Twenty-five years later, during a chat with one of my customers, I was told another story that really struck a chord. He had been to a bar in New York and had experienced the most fantastic service. The bar staff were genuinely good people and high quality in their ability to communicate. He felt they were so unique that he asked one of the waitresses about them. He was told that she had bought her 'shift' from the owner of the bar. She was, in effect, a businesswoman, and she saw the job as her business. The tips she could make from her shift far outweighed the cost of buying the 'franchise', and it was her responsibility to make the customers happy. Therefore, providing high-quality, fast service was her priority. Instead of costly staff overheads, the bar owner had people selling his drinks and snacks with a level of professionalism that set him apart from the competition.

When I was given the opportunity to share my thoughts with you in a book, I felt great emotion about this. My constant driver is 'this book must help people be emotionally and financially wealthier'. That is the intention with which I have written this book. Throughout its pages there will be emotional and practical advice drawn from eleven years' experience of building a social business network and observing and supporting over 500,000 people every month who all want to feed their families and create security for their future.

Reading this book should be an enjoyable experience. You may want to highlight some thoughts that you read, but overall, my ideas should just flow into your mind, your heart and your soul, and help you to see how to leverage the great new world that is being created around you. Most importantly of all, you should also learn how to be a part of it. This book should feel like a conversation with a good friend.

I am an emotional person. This does not mean I am not financially motivated. I am a business person and I have taken my business life very seriously. I have created a great global business with two colleagues, Thomas Power and Glenn Watkins. We know how to help people make money.

I want this journey of learning to give you a warm feeling of what is achievable. By the end you should be ready to immerse yourself in a new world that has been created around you and is waiting for you to become a part of it. I will teach you why, I will show you how, I will share stories and I will care for you throughout this journey. This world is becoming a better place to be part of and you will be equipped to maximize the potential that exists for you in it.

Know Me, Like Me, Follow Me is about getting you online and showing you that being online is not about the technology – it is about the people. The technology is purely an enabler to help you find the right people and knowledge and ensure the right people find you.

At the core of my writing is a philosophy regarding the direction in which the world is moving and I support this with practical tips on how to understand and leverage this. If you are task driven you will create a job list of sites to go to and things to do. If you are people driven you will look at your network and the people you know in a different light and see how to leverage your connections in this new world. If you can be both people driven and task orientated, a rare breed, you will see a whole new world unfold and find that this new world will provide a rich experience for you, enabling you to unlock a potential you have inside that you can now share with the whole world.

WHO AM I?

I am a forty-five-year-old mother of three, married to my business partner, Thomas. Thomas and I are the owners of Ecademy, which we started in 1998 with our business partner and CEO, Glenn Watkins. Eleven years on, Ecademy is financially strong, has a brand that is deeply valued and protected by its members, is loved by many and has created a new way of doing business that hundreds of thousands of people around the world benefit from. I spend 100 per cent of my working life helping business people be more connected and more successful. I don't do this on a one-to-one basis. I have created a place where people achieve this themselves and with one another.

As a mother I have been able to bring up my children with only a small amount of external help – five hours a week from an incredible lady who has been with us on our journey since 1995. Thomas and I owe a great deal to Susan Kingham for her love and support, and our children adore her. I have a great relationship with my children and my husband. Now before you reach for a bucket, you will learn that this has not been achieved without pain, sacrifice and pure determination. It has all been achieved because of developments in the online world and the technology that enabled our site to develop and provide amazing tools and because, for some unknown reason, I could feel the change that was happening in the world before it became apparent to many.

CREATING A NEW BUSINESS

In 1997 I was at home with my three very young children, aged six months, three and five years old. I was no longer working in industry, I was a full-time mother. Thomas had just sold his business and was working freelance helping e-commerce companies from the USA enter the UK and European markets. Working for yourself is great – no one can fire you, you manage your own time, you learn to take the rough with the smooth and hope that by the end of each year you have come out more smooth than rough.

What is not easy is being everything to all people in

business and I noticed that the energy and enthusiasm Thomas had when he started soon reduced, as he was doing more of the business tasks that he disliked than the ones he liked. I also noticed that as a well-connected man he was becoming a human switchboard. Connecting people with one another was becoming a huge part of Thomas's life. I have to admit now that on occasions I became frustrated by the number of times he had meetings with people who to me seemed irrelevant. I would ask, 'What has this person got to do with the projects you have?' Thomas would patiently reply, 'Nothing, but I like them and want to help them.'

In early 1998, I read a book called *The Celestine Prophecy*. Ironically, this was recommended to me by one of the people that I couldn't understand Thomas meeting up with! I have a lot to thank Les Francis for. Something from this book struck a powerful chord inside me. I felt a great feeling of relief after reading the thoughts that James Redfield had about the future and how people would connect with one another at a greater level of communication. They really inspired me. I then went back to my usual, more practical reading and read a book called *Permission Marketing*, by one of my favourite writers and marketers, Seth Godin.[2] *Permission Marketing* had a great impact on my business head. Seth Godin's thoughts of transforming strangers into friends and friends into customers were both simple and brilliant. Reflecting on this now it is clear to me why I created a global network of business people and why it is so successful for those that participate and become part of the community.

Throughout this early part of my journey three elements came together:

1. Observing Thomas and his quest to create a personal brand and take responsibility for his future.

2. Reading *The Celestine Prophecy* and being enlightened by the fact that you could accelerate the power of synchronicity and realize that coincidences may have a deeper meaning.
3. Reading *Permission Marketing* and understanding the power of turning strangers into friends and that these friends may become influencers in your business life.

I decided in a flash that I needed to connect business people across the world and help them connect, support and adapt to a changing world. And so the concept of Ecademy was born.

SOCIAL MEDIA AND BUSINESS

When I started Ecademy, I started it with enormous emotional drivers. It was at a time when the world was obsessed with the technical tools that the internet was offering, it seemed that there were new tools every day to seduce the vulnerable and connect the powerful. I sound ridiculously cynical about this, but I could not see how the technology was actually enriching lives. I could not view technology as anything other than an enabler. It is people that make up this world and technology can only help, it is not the solution. To some extent it reminded me of the 1980s when everyone became obsessed with the Time Manager – a portable filing system that could fit in your briefcase or handbag and could supposedly change your life. I was sent on a course to learn how to manage my time more effectively and what they taught me was 'change your life to suit this new system'. How absurd is that? Time Manager started to work for me when I used the system to support my life. This is what I want to help you understand – the online world will support you, teach you, help you adapt, connect you to amazing, fun and weird people, but at all times it is about the people, not the technology. The online world can be a personal solution for you, your place to be you and for others to like, respect and want to get to know you more.

The following chapters will take you on a journey – through understanding the context of *why*, to being able to know the *how*. The journey is a combination of marketing, philosophies, business processes and technology enablers. By the end you will have a plan and an understanding and be able to equip yourself to deal with the twenty-first-century business challenges and, critically, you will have a network around you that will feed you because you feed them.

The following quote from *The Celestine Prophecy* is one of the factors that inspired me to start a social network for business people.

For half a century now, a new consciousness has been entering the human world, a new awareness. It begins with the heightened perception of the way our lives move forward. We notice chance events and meetings that occur just at the right moment, and bring forward just the right individuals to suddenly send our lives in a new and important direction. Once we understand what is happening and how to maximize its occurrence in our lives, human society will take a quantum leap into a whole new way of life – creating a culture that has been the goal of history all along. When a large group experiences these coincidences or serendipity, this can cause a transformation in human nature.

CHANGE IS ALL AROUND YOU

I wonder if you can feel the change that is happening in the world. I don't mean have you read it or if you hear people talking about it, I mean do you actually feel it in your bones, in your conscious waking hours and your subconscious thinking hours? It is a good change and I am very excited about it. I could feel it starting to happen twelve years ago. I could sense that the material needs of people were being slowly overtaken by their need to belong, to care about and support others. It was certainly less visible than it is now, but it was there all the same. I am very positive about the change. Prosperity, growth, wealth and success still exist and are important, but can be achieved in a way we can all be a part of. We are learning that being liked and trusted is critical to survival and the more that people can trust us the greater the rewards. One by one people are creating and making the change. When this spreads and people, en masse, start to absorb the changing philosophies, then we will see a change that, as James Redfield says 'has been the goal of history all along'.

OUR NEEDS REMAIN THE SAME

We know that each of us wants to feel safe, secure, to trust others and be trusted, to prosper and to develop. In 1943, Abraham Maslow wrote his famous paper on the hierarchy of human needs, *A Theory of Human Motivation*.[3] In this paper Maslow created a list of needs, in a hierarchical order, that started with basic needs and grew to the more sophisticated needs that we develop as our basic needs are provided for. The Western world provides an economy whereby most basic, physiological needs are covered; most of us have water, clean air to breathe and food.

The next level of need is for security, employment, family, health, property and morality. Maslow calls these the 'need for safety'. Third, is the 'need for belonging', provided through friendship, intimacy and, of course, family. Family appears in both the need for 'security' and for 'belonging', as the 'family' provides a solution to both these needs. This is interesting when we can see all around us how in the Western world the family is breaking down. Once our basic needs, our needs for security and our sense of belonging are fulfilled, we lift our desire to a need for 'self-esteem', i.e. to achieve, to be respected and to have others we respect around us. The twentieth century was focused on this need for self-esteem. People chased the dream of achievement – some achieved it, others are still dreaming and hoping. It is the dreamers and hopers that concern me, as they have not moved beyond simply wishing for a better future for others and few take real action. We do see that some of today's richest people have already made the transition to considering others. Bill Gates is a great example of someone who is giving his wealth to enhance healthcare and reduce extreme poverty through his Bill & Melinda Gates Foundation.

Something that I was told once – forgive me for not knowing the source – had a profound impact on me. It was, 'You are not a millionaire until you have given a million away.' What a great goal that is. A rare few have had the mindset and the money to act in such a philanthropic manner, but those that commit to giving and caring for others have reached the peak of Maslow's hierarchy of needs and display acceptance, morality and a lack of prejudice. As a result, such people can be more creative and focused on problem-solving. This peak of human desires and needs is what Maslow calls self-actualization.

TURNING MASLOW ON HIS HEAD

My observation of this period of time in which we live is that Maslow now needs to turn his theory on its head for the Western world and state that self-actualization, in the past a luxury for those who have already achieved their basic needs, is actually now one of the first needs we must embrace. Maslow chooses the following words for self-actualization – morality, creativity, spontaneity, problem-solving, lack of prejudice, acceptance of facts. Today I can state that those that place these values at the centre of their lives are more likely to feed themselves, have shelter, have a sense of belonging and be part of a well-nourished and functional family than those that only dream of being like this.

REBOOTING THE WORLD

Over the last three to four decades we have witnessed insatiability for more. More money, more beauty, more possessions. Bigger, faster, stronger. What a tough world to live in. How can any one of us really achieve contentment among these values? It has been impossible to be noticed without broadcasting success, talking *at* people, telling people about your latest purchase and plans for your large house, or how successful your children are. It is frightening to be part of this and it has been all around us. We have been absorbing this even if we have refused to be part of it. The saddest part of this is that people are now more isolated, lonely and confused than ever. In focusing on our own needs for esteem we have actually lost the fundamental needs for belonging, community and true friendship. But the world is rebooting, a ctl-alt-dlt on the hard disk of greed, and that is why I am so positive about the future. Once we remove greed, we can all thrive.

I have spent eleven years meeting thousands of people – a 'professional networker' some could call me. I have met people who have made my hair stand on end both in pleasure and in horror. I have also listened to the most stimulating speakers and performers on stage who have delivered complete rubbish through hype, lies, storytelling, raising expectations and increasing greed.

Over the last eleven years my husband and I have lost our family home in order to invest in Ecademy. I have worked in my sons' school for free to keep them there while building Ecademy. We have never lost our belief that the online social world will be the future of business. Now we are seeing it everywhere.

What I have learnt about human nature is if you are honest with others and if you show your vulnerabilities, then people open up and tell you the truth. This is why I have known that the bubble was going to burst. People have been living a lie and projecting it to the external world, thinking that what others need to see is wealth and possessions to be valued. Thank goodness that is changing.

I have attended hundreds of different business networking events, with hungry people looking for their next meal, being taught the sixty-second elevator pitches. I am known for my dislike of this. How ridiculous is it to teach others how to broadcast what they do in sixty seconds in the hope that they will be able to sell to you in the future? Equally, the assertive distribution of business cards at events does not make anyone trust or like you. People have had enough of broadcasting and listening to others talk about themselves. We are all saturated in other people's marketing messages. What we all want is friendship – people we can trust at home and in business. We want to know who you are, not what you do. If you are one of these people who brandishes your business card, who looks for what you can get from a person rather than what you can give to them, if you self-promote, then stop! Start being a friend to others – this will change your life and will build you a personal brand that will feed you forever.

If you say to yourself 'I don't believe this' or 'I don't have time for this', then read this again and again and again until you see the writing on the wall in front of you. The world is changing. The same habits cannot be repeated in this century as the last. Your reputation as a 'good guy' is more critical than whether you can display your wealth. No one is interested in your possessions any more. This is not what impresses people.

Let me ask you to do this. Take some time to think about who you like to spend time with and write down their names. Now write down why you like spending your valuable time with them. Perhaps you will have written down some of these words:

They listen, they show an interest in me, they offer help, I can trust them, they are stimulating, they know what they are talking about, they don't waffle, they understand their values, they know how to contribute at the right time, they know other good people . . . the list goes on.

Now write down some of the reasons you value yourself and your key characteristics. Be honest. Why do people like you?

Why do you get a call out of the blue from people? Why are you so popular? Why do opportunities come to you when you need them . . . or do they?

So many people are worried about showing a weak side, independently managing their lives. The British stiff upper lip is not only British now, it is a global expectation. If you are like this, then are you proud of your independent nature? Are you happy that you can survive without anyone else helping you? Do you spend each day climbing up tough mountains or would it be good to take gentle walks with friends and enjoy the view?

Your future will be based increasingly on who you are and what you contribute. This is Maslow's self-actualization level, i.e. the peak of human needs. This is displayed through your ability to help and accept others. Creating friends around you rather than acquaintances, being interested in many things not just money and being socially compassionate should be your focus.

Many people are suffering adversity through the economic situation we find ourselves in. Some may think that as a result they will move their values into being hunters and increase the need for a competitive spirit and a 'me-me' set of values. However, the reverse is happening. There is an abundance of sharing and of caring, and those that move themselves into a set of values based on those around them and not just on themselves will be the successful people in the twenty-first century.

Your personal brand, i.e 'who' you are, will be the key factor in determining your ability to feed yourself and your family. You cannot procrastinate. This is the future *now*. The online world is enabling people to share, care and help others across cultures and races, all using their individual styles and contributing in their own unique way. While this book will teach you how to use the online world to create your brand, I cannot teach you about the technology without you absorbing and making changes in your attitudes to others if you feel that you have not given time for this in your life so far. Your future is not about you, it is about those around you. This represents a new set of business philosophies and values. Once you understand the changing world and you agree to adapt, be true to yourself, be yourself and perhaps redefine yourself, the technology will then serve you and you can be its master.

CHAPTER 2

A CHANGING WORLD – THE INDIVIDUAL CAPITALIST

IN DECEMBER 2008, while I was preparing my mind to start writing this book, I was gathering thoughts, contacts, ideas and inspiration. I heard Julie Meyer of Ariadne Capital, and founder of First Tuesday, talk about 'individual capitalism'. It was the first time I had heard this phrase and I loved it; a spine-tingling moment that summed up exactly what the future is for us all. As I meet people socially and in business and when I speak to the self-employed or the corporate employee, one theme I consistently hear is 'I want to be in control of my life and I want to be myself.' It is tough to share your personality and be yourself when you represent a brand that is not yours, and worse still when you represent a company that does not treat people as you would like to treat them. This period of economic history will be marked by the rise of the individual. ·

The twenty-first century is about individual capitalism and the end of corporates dominating the business landscape, controlling lives and the economy. Individuals are the strongest force and the large organizations will increasingly learn how to adapt to this workforce and change their business models to the low-cost, highly flexible operations that the individual capitalist is creating. To be an individual capitalist you have to create a brand – You Ltd, You Plc – be in demand, be known and have a globally trusted name that earns you respect and feeds you. To do this, you need to know your unique contribution, your talent, your skill, your passion and your reason for getting up in the morning. Money cannot be the only motivator. Your contribution has to be what creates the heartbeat that wakes you up. Later I will address the area of 'contribution'.

In May 2009, David Cameron, leader of the Conservative Party in the UK, had the following message to share on the theme of the individual and personal responsibility. This is a copy of the words he used in an e-mail to his supporters.

> Today, in a speech to the Open University, I set out our plans for a radical redistribution of power back to the people: from the state to citizens; from Whitehall to communities; from bureaucracy to democracy. This is a massive, radical change. But I believe that through decentralization, accountability and transparency we can take power away from the political elite and hand it to the man and woman in the street.

This music is everywhere and we all now have to listen to its tune and dance to the new rhythm of opportunity.

CASE STUDY OF ECADEMY

This is my story as an individual capitalist. It is a case study for you to find empathy with and hopefully learn from my experiences, good and bad. I will share with you my drivers, fears, sacrifices and, ultimately, the business model that the co-founders of Ecademy and I created as a team. The business model, which is now a blueprint for others, was created just because it felt right and was the only way we could do it. We started with a matchbox business plan and our motto since has been 'Don't plan, just play'. It is difficult to make plans in a rapidly changing market. Plans can stifle you and stop you from listening and sensing.

Ecademy was created in 1998, a home for small business. Creating the world's first social network is a great feeling. It has certainly been a journey – a journey with no teachers, no one to learn from and no blueprint to follow. LinkedIn – the world's leading business network – was founded in 2002, MySpace in 2003 and Facebook in 2004, so there was quite a gap between our foundation and the next. I am proud of what we have created and the lives we touch. We have built Ecademy the traditional, organic way; no venture capital, but with our own money and our own sacrifices. Our market has been niche – the over thirty-fives, business owners, in all corners of the world. Our success has been due to four things:

1. The ability to understand how to manage costs.
2. The ability to adapt, sacrifice and listen.
3. The close, intimate and dedicated understanding of our members' needs.
4. Our total 100 per cent commitment to how we can contribute to the success of others.

Ecademy has never been about us. It is about our members, their lives, their ups, their downs and their needs.

What intrigues me is the dichotomy of needs when you have two conflicting groups of people to please – your shareholders and your customers. What is evident in the world today is that the shareholders have been the primary focus for many companies. I am pleased to say that our shareholders have all known that it is the customers, the members of Ecademy, that must eat first and foremost.

I wonder now if the lack of financial drive at the beginning has made Ecademy what it is. At the beginning I started Ecademy with one intention: 'Could we help business people by enabling them to connect with one another?' Eleven years on, the same message and the same intention is true. Ecademy connects business people all over the world in more than 230 countries, a staggeringly busy community all sharing knowledge, all helping one another. Every second of the day, members are posting thoughts, connecting, sharing, helping and enabling each other to have greater self-esteem, greater self-belief and greater business presence.

The dot-com industry was relatively quiet when the idea came into my head and we started up in 1998. I had no idea that we were entering a period of massive change and massive company valuations. I was a business person when I started, but I was not an entrepreneur. I was not an individual capitalist, I did not use the internet. I had a lot to learn.

At the beginning, six months into the life of Ecademy, my husband Thomas and our two fellow directors, one of whom remains with us to this day, Glenn Watkins (who runs the business as our CEO), and I, found ourselves being courted by the 'City'. We were advised that we could be millionaires overnight and were blinded by the possibilities to find enormous investment in our idea. At the time, the venture capitalists were obsessed with scalability (they still are) and they could not understand the thought of people being the most important aspect of what the internet world could deliver. They saw online retail and the movement of products and services through this new medium, with its new distribution chain, as the only place to invest. E-commerce was a revolution. To this day it is incredible to see the effect it is having on the economic world. In 2009, the venture capitalists have been proven right. The low-cost, highly efficient business models that they could see in the 1990s have succeeded on the whole, but they are bringing about mass unemployment and reduction in property values and we are only on the cusp of this change.

Several years later, the venture capital world did see the merits of people – Facebook, LinkedIn, MySpace, Twitter, Socialmedian, Flickr, YouTube. There are many fantastic success stories that are all changing lives and, as I will discuss later, changing the way business is being found and conducted.

In March 2000, without venture capital, and with a firm belief that we needed to raise money to grow in scale, our only option was to float on the stock market. I remember finding this quite grotesque, embarrassed by the valuation that was being placed on a business that had hardly even traded. One night I was lying next to Thomas in bed and I couldn't sleep. I said to him that I was so uncomfortable that at thirty-six, with very little contribution to this world, I was now being personally valued at £22 million. The business had a small income from some consulting and sponsorship of our events, and yet people were going to be encouraged to invest their hard-earned money into this idea, as that was all it was at the time, an idea. Right time, right place, but zero contribution, just the hope that one day we would change lives – was that really enough?

I am happy to say that I can now sleep at night, soundly, because we didn't float on the stock market. The dot-com bubble burst and our honour remained intact and thankfully, the business that we love has kept growing due to real contribution and a real exchange of value and service. I must mention here a group of great people, some amazingly supportive seed investors who are still with us and have been a constant support through their understanding and lack of greed. Steve Clarke was the first investor, right at the beginning – he saw the opportunity as a commercial man, and we are grateful to him. My parents, Duff and Irene Ross, were the first seed investors, along with my brother Alasdair. All three have showed their belief throughout – my parents have always made me feel 'I can'.

The eleven years of building Ecademy have been the toughest of our lives. Twenty-five per cent of our life so far, eleven years of my forty-five years on this planet, have been spent entirely focused on one message: 'Can we help business people to be more successful?' Three people – Thomas, Glenn and I – have had the most ridiculous, unwavering belief that we are right. Blind belief, against all odds, that one day the world would see that family values and business ethics would return, that the need to be part of a community would become critical for modern business and that people would once again see that being among good people that care for one another is the only way to survive. We created a community, a business family. We all share the same ultimate intention, to help one another be more successful.

I have now shared with you the purpose, the intention. Ecademy began as a solution to a need for business people and it remains just that eleven years on. I have often said that Thomas is the brain of Ecademy, I am the heart and Glenn is the nervous system that makes it all work. The members, the community, are the heartbeat of Ecademy, without a heartbeat there would be no life.

THE ECADEMY BUSINESS MODEL

Ecademy is privately owned and sustains itself through subscription. Three per cent of our community want to use more advanced tools to be more active, connect more, blog and run groups, and that three per cent feed us through their monthly subscription payment. The rest of the community feeds one another and feeds Ecademy's 'value pool' through the sharing of knowledge and the connections. We value the whole community, each person is part of the Ecademy eco-system and their activity constantly helps the community get stronger and increases the value for everyone and for the business. Fifteen per cent of Ecademy's revenue comes from advertising and partnerships. Trying to teach the larger organizations the value of community is tough. Large organizations still want to broadcast and have not yet learnt that the twenty-first century demands engagement and conversation. They will learn, but they are learning the hard way.

The one and only reason that Ecademy still exists among a graveyard of dot-coms is because we have stayed private and have been able and motivated to reduce costs and make our own sacrifices to remain trading. We have learnt the power of having a low-cost, highly adaptive business model. We have been completely committed to our monthly formal board meetings between the three of us, we minute them and each month we pore over our costs and see where we need to reduce and where we need to increase. When the business needs money to grow, we reduce our personal incomes, on occasion to zero. For several years we barely took a salary. At one stage we had the most obscene amount of personal credit cards and bank loans just to survive and buy food. We sold our house because we could no longer pay the mortgage and we paid off the loans with our own capital. We have lived with my parents and I have worked at my sons' school for free, full-time, to keep them there. These are the things you do to keep your business strong. These learning experiences have been invaluable. We have created a low-cost business model for others to learn from, a global business with a great brand, with five people on the staff, including the three directors and no office/property costs.

Ecademy is a large organization. It has over 500 offline events a month, has a knowledge pool that is so large and high in quality that members by default are optimized on Google on the front page (subscribing members only) and operates in over 230 countries. We have over 5,000 micro social networks (clubs or groups) within Ecademy and we enjoy gaining a new member to the family every three minutes. So, with only five people on the payroll and no office, does that make us a small business or a large twenty-first-century business?

Modern business needs to be low-cost, highly adaptable and totally customer focused. As a management team of five, we are focused entirely on the customer. We listen, we communicate, we share, we discuss and we serve them. We are not managing staff, we are not managing and spending money on facilities, we are lean and we can adapt on a pin.

Two years ago I had a meeting with a senior person from the Chamber of Commerce. He had been on Ecademy for six months and wanted to meet and discuss his experience. He explained to me the difference in his experience between an online social network and a traditional network like the Chamber. He did not mention the technology aspect, to him that was irrelevant. He saw it, quite rightly, as purely an enabler, a way to achieve more, faster, but nothing more. What he told me was invaluable. He explained that in his dealings with new members of the Chamber, he saw them act out their business life in a traditional way. When they started their business they took out premises, hired staff, gave out job titles and in effect created an organization, steeped in costs; the majority traded locally. However, on Ecademy he saw a different behaviour. People worked from home (80 per cent of Ecademy's members log in from home), they did not employ staff, they created teams of people around them to deliver services when they needed them and they were global. In effect, they created a virtual business, no costs unless there was a sale against that cost.

If I look at this in terms of Ecademy, this is how we have built our business. We believe in the need for people to control their lives and have the ability to integrate their business life with their home life. Family is important if we are to create well-rounded adults of the future. Glenn Watkins' management style is to monitor the output of people that work with us, not their input. So, for example, our support team who answer questions, provide guidance and help to ensure that members remain within the ethos of Ecademy are all members of Ecademy, chosen because of their commitment to others and the reputation they have created online. They are in several places around the world to cover different time zones and they work when there is work to be done. They are highly skilled at what they do, not just intellectually, but emotionally too, and they are chosen as they have the talent, not just the skills, for their chosen task. The same applies to our team of financial advisers and bookkeepers, our web developers, led by our CTO Julian Bond and so on. I like this highly adaptable model as it ensures that those who work with us are paid for what they are good at, they see us as a client so they retain a high level of input and they do not go stale. In terms of costs, we are not paying PAYE and National Insurance and we do not have offices to house them all together so we can adapt the needs of the business against the way the costs are distributed.

Finally, and to me the most important benefit of this business model, is that we are entirely customer focused. In a traditional business organization the more you grow the further away from the customer you are. I would now be too far away from my customers to know what they want. Whereas, I spend 80 per cent of my working time communicating with our members through messages, training, speaking and over 120 meetings annually. I hear what they want, I hear their needs, their pain, their success, what is working and what we could do better. I rely on no one for my research, I am intuitively plugged in and live the lives that our members live. The empathy this gives me for my market is what keeps us strong, and this is the same for Glenn and for Thomas. We are part of our network, we are inside it. To me this is the future. Conversation by conversation, business executives must listen all the time.

WHY THE NEED FOR CHANGE?

The purpose of this book is to share my thoughts on the positive way that the world is changing and how you can adapt to share in this success that will abound. I am keen to stay off the bad news that the media likes us to read each day. However, I cannot ignore the facts and therefore have to highlight some of them. All the changes are not necessarily economic ones, and these are the ones that interest me most.

Are the changing styles and behaviours of people a result of the adversity that many are facing? Or is the need for change creating the adversity?

Let's look at some facts. I have a great man to thank for much of this input, David Smith of Global Futures and Foresight (www.thegff.com). He has provided me with excellent input regarding the changes we are currently seeing.

What is occurring in our lives is very complex. It is the merging of many factors that are all coming to a head together. I am not an economist or a politician, I see this situation simply and I witness it in my everyday life.

- The economy and its effect on people – a culture that has led to a massive level of debt and leading us to unemployment.
- The internet – a new way of connecting people to products, services and one another, providing a low-cost model for trading globally.
- Irresponsibility – people believing that if you can 'get away with your actions' then it is OK.
- The need to socialize online – due to the challenges of time and fear of the safety issues offline.

THE ECONOMY AND THE PEOPLE

We are all aware of the debt that many individuals and businesses have built up over the last ten years. The ability to take out credit has been irresponsibly easy, but many of us have been able to change our lives as a result, perhaps only for the short term. Whether we have the ability to repay it is the painful part. This ability to buy on credit has created a world of instant gratification and greed. The patience of individuals to wait for something they want has virtually gone. I remember the days when birthdays and Christmas were the times we had new things in our lives, now it is almost an everyday occurrence. This has resulted in a debt culture that has been created, globally. People have become self-indulgent and, in fact, have become risk takers, buying on credit on the assumption that they will pay it off later. This belief also brings with it massive stress and a focus on working to pay the money off. This then becomes a vicious circle of stress, whereby you forget your reasons for working. Am I working to buy something in the future that I aspire to or to pay off something that I bought in the past and now find hard to value? The latter is of course a very unrewarding situation to be in, but sadly it is the reality of many. As a result of this many are seeking a more rewarding way of working, finding ways that they can contribute to others, working to repay the debt to the lenders as well as to society. The most common phrase I hear is, 'I want purpose, I need to feel my work is making a difference.'

THE SUPPLIER WORKFORCE

The financial consequences of the last ten years have resulted in an economy that is now working to pay off debt. Unable to borrow more, over half of UK adults are clearing their debts or at least making plans to do it when they can, rather than continue to consume. This is creating a staggeringly high rate of unemployment. The director general of the International Labour Organization (ILO) stated, 'We need prompt and coordinated government action to avert a social crisis that could be severe, long lasting and global.' He said that it was 'about time that all governments of the world work in a coordinated manner to combat this phenomenon of jobless-ness'. Focusing on the need for collaboration, not com-petition, solutions need to be found to ensure that the number of unemployed people in the world does not increase by the anticipated 20 million that they estimate will happen.[4] The ILO's preliminary estimates indicate that the number of unemployed could rise from 190 million in 2007 to 210 million in late 2009. This level of unemployment or the loss of full-time, employed work is not the true picture as many people are already focusing on becoming self-employed and going freelance, in effect becoming suppliers to the same organizations that they used to work for. This is giving birth to the supplier workforce, rather than an employed one. Many of those who lose their job will have to become a supplier. National governments cannot support an unemployed population at the levels predicted. Becoming a supplier will be the only alternative for many.

There are many positives to this shift. In a survey conducted by the *Yellow Pages* in 2003, 85 per cent of those surveyed felt that in the UK the nine-to-five working culture was in decline. Almost 90 per cent agreed that their lifestyle had become increasingly twenty-four/seven, giving them flexibility to do what they wanted, when they wanted. The challenge for all was the balance of work and home.

AN AGEING POPULATION

We will all have to work and earn a living longer than our parents. The population is ageing and the state retirement age is set to rise steadily. You have to assume that you will need to create a brand around yourself that will sustain a standard of living far beyond your retirement age. Relying on a pension from an institutional fund or the government is no longer enough. Most will have to take responsibility for their own income. Consider also that the pension age is forecast to rise gradually to sixty-eight for both men and women between 2024 and 2046.[5] This means that you need to create an income that will last you longer than previous generations have been required to achieve.

Will you be employed when you are in your late fifties and sixties? Or will you need to create a client list and a network that respects you and understands your experience, your contribution and will want you to be their supplier?

THE HOMEWORKER

I have observed the homeworker for eleven years through Ecademy. Eighty per cent of those who log into Ecademy are logging in from their homes. I have learnt one great lesson as a homeworker myself. You cannot balance your life by placing the two aspects, work and home, on a set of scales. The two end up competing. However, you can integrate them and see one enabling the other. In my own life I work hard. However, I also make sure that I see my sons' rugby games, take them to school and, in the main, collect them and always cook their evening meal. If this means that I work later in the evening to complete the tasks I wanted to achieve that day then I will. Integrating my family life and my work life is critical for my well-being. Our children have travelled to Europe, the USA and Asia with us, meeting our members and understanding and contributing to Ecademy's intention. Bringing your children into your work life and helping them understand what you, as a team, are achieving and contributing, is a great way of ensuring that they do not object to you working around their lives and their lives working around your work. Transparency is a key message of my book and this transparency needs to begin at home.

Working from home is the most cost-effective way to manage your work and life. It requires a strong determination and drive to focus on your work at times, but it is the best way of managing and giving time to both your home and your work. Technology is, of course, critical if you are at home. With technology you can build your reputation, talk to hundreds of people each week, connect with thousands and when you feel isolated or need inspiration you can talk to others in your network using Skype or reach out on a social network. We all need to learn and be inspired to advance ourselves and to adapt to the changes. It is critical as a homeworker that you do not isolate yourself. Online networks are social networks and this must always be considered.

I receive many messages from members who tell me that their online world has saved their business, not purely because of the commercial and financial wins, but critically, because of their emotional needs. With isolation comes fear, loneliness and apathy. With friendship you can welcome self-esteem, self-belief and success.

THE INTERNET – THE RISE IN A NEW WAY OF DOING BUSINESS

Ironically, there are many success stories during these difficult economic times these are seen on the internet. IMRG Capgemini e-Retail Sales Index estimates an increase of 25 per cent year-on-year of e-retailing.[6] The new financial reality is creating a need for low-cost products. People are turning to the internet to save money.

I remember when e-commerce was seen as an operational decision by companies, another distribution channel, tactically treated. Only those that saw the internet as a strategic change for their business, those who created new business models around this new opportunity, this new way of doing business, have and will survive.

Our family and our business are huge users of Amazon, they are one of our main suppliers. They have never let us down, they continue to innovate and their customer service is second to none. Yet Amazon was only founded in 1994 and began trading in 1995. Launched as an online bookstore, they were not seen as a threat to most high-street retailers, but now they sell computers, hardware and software, video games, electronics, apparel, furniture, toys, shoes, the list goes on. In fact, they are a threat to every retailer – booksellers, banks, utility companies – you name it. What can they not sell now they have perfected this business model and have built trust?

A SOCIAL WORLD WHERE BUSINESS HAPPENS

I see the same challenges around the world of social networking, banging the drum as we have in the world of venture capital funds, banks and suppliers of business solutions. We have tried to help them all understand that social networking is not just another marketing channel or a new type of 'networking'. Social networks are a new way of doing business, far reaching in their ability to change the processes, structures and philosophies of the business market. Social networking is creeping up on the world and will be yet another opportunity that many will miss. Even now, among the millions of users of social networks – the children, the teenagers, the businessmen and -women, the business owners – few see what it actually is. Most view it as a method to swap electronic business cards or broadcast a message. Those that see it as a collaborative, low-cost solution to their business, economic and social needs and build a global reputation inside the social networks and embed their businesses and stakeholders within them are the winners of the future. Social networks are not just for teenagers, they are a social world where business happens.

IRRESPONSIBILITY BECOMES RESPONSIBILITY

By the end of this book you will understand that there is a positive change and that it is happening within social networks and you will know what to do to ensure you are part of it. But for now I have to focus on a negative, on the third factor that I believe has had an effect on the world. It is irresponsibility.

There seems to be a vast number of people who believe that as long as their actions do not affect them directly, then everything is OK. Believing that the consequences of their actions stay under the radar and go unnoticed and are not linked back to them gives them some sort of comfort. So long as their personal wealth remains strong by focusing on their own needs everything is fine. Recently we have seen many questionable practices within large corporations, banks and governmental institutions that highlight this lack of responsibility. Sadly, when people see authority figures acting in this way they have in the past almost condoned their actions as individuals. To me this is gross irresponsibility as a member of the human race. We all have to take responsibility for one another, for our future and the mistakes of the past. We are all connected and must take this connectedness more seriously in order for this world to make the positive changes that I believe can happen.

Being connected is a reality now, no one can work in isolation and everyone's actions are transparent and obvious. I do not mean solely on the internet either, your reputation is far more obvious than that. In all that you do, your reputation, attitude and actions can have an effect on your future just by your being. I will cover this later when I talk about emotional wealth and how this affects your ability to achieve financial wealth.

Irresponsibility has been fuelled by the rules and controls that have been placed on people and as a result these rules have become the gauge of what is right and wrong. I have always been amazed when people say 'I was lucky, I didn't get stopped for drinking and driving and I was over the limit.' It is as though the legal system has become the barometer for what is right rather than our own set of values. Getting in a car and driving with alcohol in your system could kill you, and worse still, could kill an innocent person. The other day I used an automated payment system in a food store. When I saw that the bill was less than expected I realized I had failed to pay for a large piece of beef. Of course I queued up and paid. I was told by the cashier that my behaviour was very rare, that many people think that they have got away without paying and leave the shop. They think that was the shop's mistake, so tough on them and lucky me. That is stealing, no matter what way you look at it.

The danger of systems, of processes and of controls is that people stop taking responsibility for their actions. They forget their own values and they start to act in a herd-like manner, forgetting that every action they take and every thought, word and intention actually does have an effect on someone else. Later I discuss this with regard to contribution and what you emit into the world. For now, let's consider the wider impact of a world based on personal gain.

We all know that the stock market has become a very wealthy environment for many. Transferring shares from one person to another or one organization to another has made many individuals extremely rich. I mentioned earlier my personal experience when I was valued at £22 million pounds, not based on my contribution, but the attractiveness of my shares. Ultimately, in the e-commerce, dot-com era, the bubble burst because the money being pumped in was based on an assumption that there would be a return on investment. However, in the majority of cases there was no return, as the return was reliant on acquisition rather than the way the capital employed was used to grow real value. The financial sectors and the internet industry have been guilty of this, and now the correction is taking place. In the end, the world corrects itself when values conflict. Financial wealth can only be measured by an equal or greater contribution to others.

What is happening in the world now, through the growth in internet usage, is that your actions are becoming increasingly transparent. In the past, individuals were protected by the brand of the company they worked for. Poor service, uncaring attitudes towards clients, even corrupt trading, trading when insolvent or misrepresentation of a product or service did not expose any individuals. This is changing. Everyone and everything can be found, one way or another, via the internet and there is nowhere to hide. Your reputation and your past actions will be the critical factors in your ability to gain work in the future. Taking responsibility for your reputation online will be a key factor determining your income in the future. What others say about you will be your marketing. This is a great change, such an enormous opportunity for all, as who you are, the values you hold, not purely your skills, will feed you in the future.

CREATING FRIENDSHIP AGAINST THE ODDS

In 1971 a study was carried out to quantify the number of children who walked to school unaccompanied. At that time 80 per cent of seven- to eight-year-olds made this journey. By the 1990s, this had steadily declined until only 9 per cent of seven- to eight-year-olds were walking to school unaccompanied by an adult. In a more recent report carried out by the Goodchild Inquiry it was discovered that only two-thirds of British children aged eight to ten had ever visited a park or a shop unaccompanied, and one-third stated that they never played outside without an adult present. This level of overprotection meant that fewer teenagers aged sixteen had a trusted best friend than they would have achieved twenty years ago.[7]

Socializing is crucial to children. It is how they learn, how they share and how they build their reputation and their personal brand. Being part of a community and having groups of friends around them teaches children independent thinking away from their parents. Society needs this. I am happy to say that a solution was found for children, or perhaps by children, in the form of MySpace, Facebook and many localized, online social networks around the world. These networks satisfy the need to trust, be known and, critically, socialize with people they like.

I have watched the online behaviour of my children with such awe and respect. I have learnt so much from them that I have been able to apply to and teach business people. It is utterly incredible what children can do to stay in touch with their friends and associates.

We have three children, twelve- and fifteen-year-old boys and a seventeen-year-old girl. 'Born digital', our children have a completely different view of the world and how we are connected.[8] Just last night I was lying on Hannah's bed and talking to her friends through her computer with her. I am still learning everyday by observing her use of technology. Anything is possible in her world. If she wants to do something she just looks for the technology to enable it. Last night she had several windows open on her screen and she could see her friends, each of them in a different house, all laughing and sharing pictures and videos, live, in real time. Stuck at home, she could still talk to as many people as she wanted to. This morning, on the way to school in the car, she was instant messaging a friend she met in California, talking about their day ahead or behind them.

It is incredible. Every day via Facebook, Skype, BlackBerry or instant messaging, Hannah, Ross and TJ are connecting with up to 100 people. Translate this into the business world and its impact is awesome.

What inspires me so much is the innocent way they are changing the world, one conversation and connection at a time. They are making friends, who will in time feed them, provide them with security and trust them with their needs. Trust, transparency and unconditional friendship will be Hannah, Ross and TJ's future, but they do not know that yet. To them they are just having fun and making friends.

So what about you? How will you feed yourself when this generation come into the business world and know the philosophies and the technology and love every minute of their day as it is just about friendship and having fun? How are you going to leverage the opportunities that exist now to create a brand online that will attract opportunities to you as an individual?

CHAPTER 3

CONTRIBUTION CURRENCY

I AM NOW GOING to take you deep inside the world of social networks. As I have said throughout, the technology is just the enabler. Once you understand the context of what is happening and the opportunities for you to create a source of income through your activities, the technology will purely be a medium through which you achieve your desired result. Do not get hung up on the technology, although you must become its master.

SUCCESS IS THE BY-PRODUCT

The most critical aspect of being a citizen in the world of social networks will be your ability to contribute to others. Success is the by-product – the result of being a team player. If you target success and have that as your only reason for spending time on a site then you will never achieve it. Success comes because of your willingness to share, listen, help and contribute to the success of others.

In many ways the online world is no different to the offline world. If you moved home into a new town or village, you would not broadcast a message from a bar stool and dish out your business card. You would find a bar or club you liked, quietly sit down, listen, observe and, when ready, you would begin to have conversations. I would guess that you would ask many questions of the existing residents. You would ask them who are the good people to know in the neighbourhood. When you needed a supplier, such as a decorator, electrician or plumber, you would ask for recommendations. The supplier who has a good reputation would be offered to you, due to trust and respect for how he/she has contributed to helping others when they were in need. It all seems so obvious, yet why do people act so differently online? I will look at some of the dangers of broadcasting and tell you how others have offended people. I don't want you to fall down at this first hurdle. Impatience to gain a result can be the death of your reputation inside a social network.

RELATIONSHIPS FIRST, COMMERCE SECOND

I think most of us know that the best and longest-standing clients we have are people that we get on well with. Building trust, enjoying their company, understanding their challenges and caring for the whole person not just their business interests, builds a solid foundation for commerce. Building trust takes time, it has to be earned and it cannot be bought.

In the twenty-first century we are all saturated with places to go to find people with skills. The internet, especially Google, provides all we need to be able to search and find someone with the skills we are looking for. But that is not enough now; it takes more than that to feel safe when making purchasing decisions. The world of recommendations and referrals to people we trust is as old as commerce itself. The internet, however, changes the landscape by being so transparent and so readily available. What people say about you online can literally feed you. People will become your advocates and refer others to you because of the relationship they have with you, not just your skills. Your future is no longer about self-promotion. Your future happiness and financial stability will be strong because of what people say about you, not what you say about yourself.

COUGH SWEETS – MY FIRST SALE

I have a story of my first experience of achieving a sale that I want to share; it was when I was nineteen years old.

In 1983, I was fresh out of school having stayed an extra year to improve some weaker areas in my education. My goal had been to become a physiotherapist, specializing in treating children with cerebral palsy. Sadly, due to academic weakness I did not achieve this dream that I had held since the age of twelve. My life was on hold until I could find another degree course, and I was working in a bar at night and in a school during the day.

One day a lady called Barbara Allen came into the bar. She was a headhunter for the computer industry. She observed my attitude towards people and asked if I had ever considered a career in sales. I looked at her in dismay; no thought could have been further from my mind. However, she encouraged me to go for an interview for a telesales position at a computer distributor. She had motivated me by the opportunity to earn lots of money to make my passage through university easier. I was shocked to be offered the job at the interview. I am not sure what they saw that gave them the idea that I would be suited to the cut-and-thrust world of computer distribution.

Before I was welcomed into the company they sent me to a telesales training course in Wales, a place I had never been to. I remember the terrifying journey. I was quite sheltered at nineteen, and still living at home. I will never forget the feeling of being out of my depth, utterly shocked that I had created this experience, based on the belief of Barbara Allen that I was a natural salesperson. It will make you laugh to know that I actually thought telesales was selling telephones, which indicates how far I was from the world of business.

The training course was one of the worst experiences of my life. Being told to role play was like being back at school and learning lines of Shakespeare. I felt like a loser and could not wait to get home. Nothing went in and, in fact, I could not tell you a thing about that three days apart from the lonely nights in an old hotel. I also remember I was away over Valentine's Day – what bad luck was that?

When I returned to the office I was greeted very kindly, given a phone, a list of computer dealers and told to 'get selling'. I was given some product training, which I treated in the same way as revising at school for exams. There was no context to what I was being taught, that is, understanding the value of a dot matrix printer over a daisywheel printer – someone save me! My lipstick became my friend and each time I lifted the phone to make a cold call, script in front of me, my lips grew fatter and fatter. Sadly, most of the calls I made were pretend, I didn't actually dial a number for two weeks.

One day I was brave and asked to speak to the decision maker. Roland Hewlin was his name. This was a turning point in my life.

Roland answered the phone. I could tell he had a sore

throat as his voice was husky. Immediately, I felt for him and my first reaction was to say that I was sorry he wasn't feeling well and that I would not disturb him today. He laughed and asked me who I worked for and told me that he used to buy from us and had moved his business, because of price, to an alternative distributor. I insisted that now was not the time for me to 'sell' to him and I wished him well.

That day, at lunchtime, while buying my lunch I noticed some cough sweets on the counter. I bought them and sent them to Roland with a little note saying that I hoped he was getting better. There was no motive, it just felt right.

Three days later a call was passed to me and down the phone came a list of computer equipment that Roland was ordering. It turned out to be the biggest order we received that week. I wrote it all down, thanked him profusely and told him I was very happy that he was feeling better. He then taught me the greatest lesson of my life. He had placed the order with me because of who I was, not who I worked for, nor in fact because I was the cheapest. He just *knew* he could trust me. This is when I knew I could fly, because I could control my destiny. If it was about who I was, then that was one thing I could control in my life.

I stayed at this company for a while and then built my career for four years elsewhere, still within the IT industry but for three other companies. Four years later I returned to my first employer as a director. At twenty-three I had eighty-plus people in my team. I travelled to many countries on conferences with our suppliers, I had a high standard of living and the best bit was that I was never motivated by the money. The status meant very little to me – what mattered was whether my team were growing in emotional and financial wealth and whether the company had a good reputation in the market. Thomas, my husband, met me while I was working there and he still finds it hilarious how little I actually knew about business, but somehow, I knew what mattered. The people.

VALUE EXCHANGE

Life was simpler in the 1980s. It was enough to know how to be kind and helpful to a customer. Posters donned office walls proclaiming 'The Customer is King' and training courses were sold teaching people that serving your customer was the most critical part of your business process. This remains true today, but now there is another level – the customers who pay nothing to access you or consume your services. How do you feel about giving away your ideas, thoughts and services for free?

Several years ago, a couple of years into building Ecademy, I learned a great lesson, that of 'value exchange'. At the time we were valuing our members based on whether they paid a subscription to use the site. This is a traditional view of customers and business. Building the business organically and risking our own personal money meant that we wanted sales. This is what 'funded Ecademy'. It was tough to value those who used the site for free and as a result we did not allow free members to do much on the site. Basically, they could read content and they could have a profile, but that was all. We gave them a very passive right of way.

In time, we began to realize that these people added value to our business that was not based on a financial exchange, there was a value associated with contribution. I call this 'contribution currency'. Since I have recognized this my mind has overflowed with thoughts around this subject. Learning to contribute and understanding your contribution is the first step to building an online brand and creating a great network around you.

In the case of a social network your contribution is how you share information, provide help and provide connections to others. This requires you to be an unconditional giver, not a taker. Many fear the time this will take, however, if this becomes second nature to you and you learn the best, most time-efficient ways to use the technology then it can be a few words, a forwarding of a link and you will have advocated and helped someone else.

CARING AND SHARING

The impact of this new world is far reaching, beyond our ability to comprehend. I can only begin to take you on the journey but once you dive in and experience it, then you will know for yourself. It is like trying to tell you how amazing my Christmas was. It is too difficult to pass on the atmosphere, the love, the surprises and the togetherness. Telling you where I went, who I was with, what I gave and received is just information. The important part of an experience is what you feel – your joy, your energy, your peace of mind. Being connected and having people wanting to connect with you has to be about the emotional part of you. If not, then it is just a utility, just a drive in the car.

UNCONDITIONAL GIVING

Last December, Hannah, our seventeen-year-old daughter was preparing for very important exams. She came home from her last day at school before the Christmas holiday and told me, very firmly, that this year Christmas was on hold. She was going to enjoy the actual day of Christmas, but apart from that she was revising. With a four-foot pile of books by her side I could tell she was serious about this. Her goal was to reduce all those books into ten word-processed documents, all colour-coded, mind-mapped and simple to digest. By the end of the Christmas period she would be prepared for her two months of exams, with only these documents as her aid.

She did it. Three weeks later she emerged happy and excited that she was going back to school, ready for her exams. She set off with a big smile on her face. At 4 p.m. that day she walked back up the drive looking sad, frustrated and not the picture of joy I expected. She told me that all of her friends were panicking and that the teachers were angry because the majority of the class had been away, partying, skiing or generally relaxing. Now the next couple of weeks would be tough while everyone tried to prepare.

The adult in me, born in the 1960s, wanted to punch the air and say, 'Well done, darling, you are ahead of the game', but I could tell that would be inappropriate. Hannah went upstairs. A couple of hours later she came down for dinner with a smile back on her face and with her usual zest for life. I ask her what had changed. What she said has had such an impact on me.

Hannah had sent all her friends the ten documents that she created. I looked at her in shock and asked her if she was not annoyed that she had sacrificed her three weeks of fun, while others had not cared about their work. She replied, 'No, Mum, now we are all at the same place and tomorrow we can go forwards together.' This is a twenty-first-century example of collaboration. This is the philosophy of putting others first, sharing and caring, and using technology to embrace the needs of others and provide solutions for them. Hannah, and all other children like her, are building a network, creating a reputation and changing the world, one by one. They will come out of their education with far more than just qualifications. Others will know their personality, know whether they can be trusted, know their passions and be able to connect them to anyone they need, anywhere in the world.

In the future, CVs will include the size of the applicant's network, the names of the online groups they chair and the words that others use to describe them. Who they are will feed them and who they know will feed others that they care for. This is the future and this is what I want to teach you to be able to do.

PROJECTING OUTWARDS

I have learnt many things in my lifetime and the greatest lesson for me was when I could see the happiness I could have when I looked at the world through other people's eyes. To look at what they need, understanding how I could best contribute at that moment in time, projecting my intention outwards rather than inwards. Rather than seeing what I could gain, I could look at what I could contribute.

This is nothing to do with a desire to be liked, to care or to even want to help. It is born from a level of empathy that allows me to switch my thinking into someone else's mind and see how they feel at the moment that I am with them. In a way it is easier to ask questions, find out about others and learn about their life, and it is often much more rewarding than focusing on your own.

The reason this has been my saviour is that time and time again when life has been tough, when I am stretched to a level of stress or capacity beyond my self-belief, as soon as I look for an opportunity to help others my emotional state changes. When I feel someone else's relief and joy, when I contribute something to them, my bank of self-belief and happiness grows.

It is said that there is no such thing as a selfless act and I entirely agree with this. Whenever you help others you gain. I do not mean in a 'pay it back way' or even in a 'pay it forward' way, I mean at that very moment, instantly, you experience success.

Let's explore this. At the beginning of my book I talked about Maslow and his hierarchy of needs. Above your need for food, shelter, security and love, is the need for self-esteem. Check Wikipedia and it states that 'self-esteem reflects a person's overall evaluation or appraisal of his or her own worth'.[9] Self-worth is critical to your ability to feel that someone will value you enough to give you money for your knowledge and skills. So many times I have seen the transformation in business people when they grasp this and realize that by helping others they actually help themselves. I have to tell you about a turning point in my life that illustrates this.

When I was young I lived in a quiet village. I am the youngest of four children and once I was ten, my brother and sisters were making lives of their own. While I have the most fantastic parents, living in a quiet village without a busy family atmosphere did make me fairly lonely. Unfortunately school was not a great deal better as I never felt I fitted in. While my peers were hugely into riding horses and many 'country activities', I did not do these things at weekends, so friendships were tough. I don't want to paint a picture of unhappiness at all, I was happy, but I was lonely at times and I didn't have a great sense of being valued.

One day a new family moved in next door. Their son,

Toby, was five years younger than me and had cerebral palsy. Toby and I grew to be very close. I loved going to see him after school and always thanked his mum, Carol, for letting me come over. It was not until I was an adult, in fact a mother myself, that I realized that this must have been a good thing for her too. I helped him eat, kept him company, read to him and laughed with him, and this must have given Carol some respite. Carol introduced me to his school and in my holidays I went there and helped out with the other children.

Five years ago, in my forties, I was asked to do a talk for a charity and the host asked me to prepare a story from my past that changed my life. Sitting on the train to Manchester, a four-hour journey, I thought hard about this and then I remembered Toby. It was at that point that I realized that Toby changed my life. It was because of Toby I believed I had significance, I could see a way that I could contribute to others and for the first time in my life I received a feeling that I was truly valued. I am eternally grateful to Toby and his mother Carol for allowing me into their lives and creating a place where my self-esteem could grow.

We have been plagued by the notion that having money and being financially successful is the route to valuing yourself. It is not. Emotional wealth is far, far more important. What is so interesting is that when you are emotionally wealthy, the money starts to flow. The reason? Because you become more attractive to know as a person, it is as simple as that.

APPLYING THIS TO SOCIAL NETWORKING

Social networks are communities; they are full of people, all with different needs, fears, skills and knowledge. These people will have a mixture of emotions and a mixture of intellects, be emotionally strong and emotionally weak and financially strong and financially weak. This is the real world.

You must assume that you have the talents and skills to fulfil the needs of many of the people that live inside these social networks. If not, then what is your value? What is your contribution?

First of all, let me tell you, you have a lot of value to others. You have been on this earth for many years. You have listened, read, shared and experienced many things that the rest of us haven't. You may also have educated yourself to a high level and you will have contributed to the success of a company or individuals while on this earth. What you may not know is how to articulate your value, or perhaps you have not discovered what that value is and you are at a point in your life where you are searching and discovering.

There is no point in knowing your value and proudly stating that it is only given if paid for. That world no longer exists. That world relied on fewer people being as clever as you, it relied on fewer people being able to afford marketing that told people how clever they were. Now your value is based on others talking about you.

The individual capitalist, YOU, is now able to have hundreds of conversations and contribute in thousands of ways that get you noticed. Being noticed and being found is your goal now. This means getting rid of those hang-ups you have about spam (unsolicited e-mails). It means being willing to share your knowledge freely, it means letting people know you want to be contacted. It means putting all barriers you have created to protect yourself away, because if you fear people knowing you exist and have knowledge that could help them, you will not have any friends online. You need those friends, as those friends will be your meal ticket.

Remember, by feeding others, you will feed yourself.

Later, in chapter seven I am going to talk about why you need a large network, why you must accept contacts from random people you meet and why you must be transparent in order to be trusted. You can scan forwards and read that now if you need some comfort about what I am saying or trust me a little longer and let me continue your journey.

DISCOVERING YOUR VALUE

I have shared with you that your value is what will create your opportunities and bring people to you. Let's explore your value to others. I have to ask you a few questions to bring out some of the thoughts you have at the moment.

1. Do you care whether others succeed?
2. Does it matter to you if others are finding life tough?
3. Do you fear people copying you or stealing your customers?
4. Do you view people as competition?
5. Do you only answer messages from strangers if you can see the benefit to you of knowing them?
6. Do you like helping people find answers to their questions?
7. Do you see value in your network of contacts for other people? Is it great when people thank you for your help?

I have chosen these questions to highlight a mix of experiences you will have when you immerse yourself in social networks. A lot of noise will be going on, a lot of information will pass by you, and in order to see how you can contribute you have to understand your value to others.

Your value is a number of things. Who you know, what you

know, how fast you react, how many networks you are on, how wide you can reach out into a network and how deep you can go to know the answer to someone's question.

Critically however, your value is not just your knowledge and skills; it is your intention, your reason for being in the network and your contribution to others. Once you know this, then you will know that your contribution is not about what you are selling, it is how well you can help people who need help, how fast you can connect them to what they need.

This is why anyone inside a network can be successful, because it is based on their intention of helping and sharing, not based on their particular way of making money. If you purely look at how you can find the people that will make you money you will spend a huge amount of your time searching and not finding. If you treat your time on the networks as a way of demonstrating your ability to share and connect others to information, others in turn will bring the right people to you, you will no longer have to search for them. Hooray for the death of cold calling!

To stress this one more time, your value is your intention to solve the needs of others. It is who you are not what you are. 'What' enables you to cut an invoice. 'Who' will bring the customer to you.

INTENTION

I have spent eleven years helping business people through Ecademy. My intention from when I wake up until I sleep, through answering messages, speaking, training, writing and looking at ways our site can be better, is how can we help business owners be emotionally and financially wealthier?

My intention is more powerful than the actions I do each

day. Somehow it drives me, keeps me focused and allows me to accept information and people into my life, just because I trust my instinct and I trust the energy that flows from me towards people. I know that when I meet someone who needs something, by connecting them to a person or a piece of information that helps them, I am achieving my intention. I know who I want to partner and collaborate with because I look for people with similar intentions.

In Chapter four I am going to explain how to attract people towards you and how to be a magnet. I have to introduce the area of intention first, because if you are not clear about your intention then you cannot send out your messages or contribute with relevance. This is why people are worried about random connections and are fearful of letting strangers into their lives. Without creating a sense of purpose and understanding around you, random connections will remain exactly that. Creating a wider set of ideas of what you want to contribute, based around your skills but focused on the goals of who you want to help, will provide those contacting you with a wider net to help you, advocate you and connect others to you.

FINDING A SHARED INTENTION WITH SOCIAL NETWORKS

Above I explained the intention of Ecademy, and I know that this intention is shared among the whole community. People know that this intention provides permission to be helpful, to be vulnerable and to provide advice freely to others. This is the heartbeat of Ecademy and it provides the energy for all to thrive within. It also creates the boundaries and the expect-ations. It is critical for any social network to create an ethos that steers behaviour, allowing people to know how to behave appropriately within the community.

I am intrigued by the intention of some social networks; I cannot quite understand what they are. LinkedIn, for example, is a social network that has its origins in the world of the corporate employee. For this reason it has inherited within its software tools one of the traits of corporate employees, and that is protection. 'Protect me from time-wasters and from people that cannot help me with my tasks.' Corporate employees have been managed by tasks. Their day is very rarely random, their diaries are filled with 'the people I must meet, the e-mails I must answer, the reports I must write'. Random interruptions are seen as annoying and irritating. For this reason the LinkedIn system does not allow random connecting whereby one stranger can contact another; it is based on introductions and trusting your network to only introduce you to people that they feel are relevant to you. This is open to massive interpretation and can only be based on where you are now, not where you are heading.

Later I will suggest some reasons why I think this system of protection is insane, and I forecast that this will change. However, my point here is that it is difficult to create an energy within the social networks that protect you from con-necting, as it is the combined energy of the whole that creates the environment for success. Filtering yourself does not allow you to absorb new information and new thoughts. It keeps you controlled and controlling. The only way to interpret the intention in this environment is 'Here I am, I am important and I will talk to you if I think you are of use to me.' I am being harsh here for a reason. I need you to understand the dangers of this world and staying locked in this old business philosophy. I want to stress here that I have enormous respect for LinkedIn and I tell everyone on my network and anyone

I train to have a profile on LinkedIn. Just be aware that its philosophies are different.

Facebook on the other hand has a good reason to protect and not allow random connections. Protecting children from random strangers is, of course, critical. What is amazing is that Facebook is adapting, and it has to. The Facebook audience is no longer just children, adults are joining in their thousands each day. I read recently that Facebook is changing and will be allowing random connections. Adapting to the needs of the adult world and the philosophies that are forming is important, but I will watch with interest how children are protected now. I have to say that it does sadden me that children have not been able to keep their own space. I guess a new social network for children will be created. My daughter tells me that she does not want to dance in the same nightclub as me and I respect that. To me her Facebook profile, along with her thoughts and pictures, are for her world, not for me to intrude into.

My personal skills are connecting people, someone else's skills may be financial or marketing or training, but the common thread is helping business owners be emotionally and financially wealthier. I have built my brand and my reputation around this intention. However, what I sell is subscription.

FOCUS ON INTENTION

I cannot feed my family unless I sell subscriptions. How dull is that? However, if I had spent the last eleven years as a subscription salesperson I would not have created a following, I would not have created a reputation. I would have been leading with the result I want, not with the intention I have.

I would have been financially motivated, not emotionally led. People see through that.

Once you understand the intention you have through your product or service you will create a following. Knowing that you intend to achieve something is like an energy force that provides a subconscious ability to achieve it. It is important for you to know what your intention is because once you know it the rest will flow. You will spot the opportunities and you will create advocates. Your intention becomes part of your brand. It enables your advocates to talk about you in a clearer way and be able to spot those people in their network that need your help. Your intention creates a vibration around you because people see, feel and witness what you can contribute to the success of others, not because you say you are good at what you do.

The interesting point for me about understanding intention is that the results seem to flow once you know it. I guess it is like 'joining you up'. Join your heart to your mind and as a result you become a more passionate person. Ask any successful entrepreneur and they will tell you that it is their passion that got them through the tough times.

It is not *what* you do that creates your success, it is *why* you do it. That clarity will give you all the tools you need to launch yourself into a social network. Being part of a network is not enough, it is the energy you put into it that creates brand YOU.

CONTRIBUTION CURRENCY WITHIN THE ECOSYSTEM

Social networks are like ecosystems, think of them as a rainforest with many habitats and species, all interdependent.

Few species actually compete, there is enough food for them all as they have adapted to their surroundings and they also accept the part they play in the food chain. The wonderful thing about an ecosystem when it is thriving is that there is abundance and it is a beautiful place.

Everything you do contributes to the success of another, providing you are doing something. Do nothing and you fade away into extinction; learn new information and meet new people and you adapt and survive.

The activities you will learn as you continue your journey through this book will be your contribution to the survival of the ecosystem, and therefore the survival of a place where you can thrive. As I'm sure you've realized by now, this is not about being a hunter and a predator, it is about being a farmer and a gatherer. This is a change in habits for many, but I can safely say that the individual hunters will not survive unless they learn to hunt in packs in a collaborative and sharing way.

WHAT YOU DO DOES NOT DEFINE YOU

While building and investing in Ecademy I found myself working for our son's school. What a fantastic experience that was. Five months after we had moved our two sons into the private schooling system, Thomas and I realized that we had made a fairly tragic financial error. We had not forecast the extra investment the business needed and our income was sacrificed. I found myself in tears in the headmaster's office. Mr Merrick was sympathetically listening to the fact that we might have to move our boys, but I was keen to find an alternative solution. Our boys know that Mr Merrick saved our bacon! The headmaster was aware that I had contributed in a voluntary way to our boys' previous school and he felt that there were some ways in which I could contribute to this school. We agreed half fees for the period that I worked for them, which was eighteen months. I worked for free during that time.

My role was girl Friday, i.e. cover the office, cover the kitchen, drive the minibus, clear up sick in classrooms (young boys are known to do this after playtime!) and basically be on hand 8.30 a.m. to 5 p.m. every day, carrying out the instructions of the headmaster. In the evenings I would come home and once homework and tea was over I would resume my role in Ecademy and answer messages, go out and speak at events and add content to the website. I cannot pretend it was not tiring at times, but the compensation was wonderful. I got to eat with my boys and I sat with their friends and I made sure I treasured every moment.

One day, feeling rather exhausted, I was changing into my suit in the staff toilets. A driver was collecting me for a speech that I was giving that evening. I felt a bit like Wonder Woman, turning around and suddenly looking different. While I was changing I was thinking about how I was enjoying the school life as much as I enjoyed speaking to large groups of adults. How could I possibly compare clearing up vomit in a classroom to standing in a large room teaching social networking? It was then that I realized that what I did was nothing to do with who I was. It did not define me. The contribution I made to the school was equal to the contribution I could make to anyone listening to my talk. What defined me was my willingness to help others, to make a crying child smile, to help a teacher in a difficult situation and to help business owners leverage the new world. Once you reach this point of discovery I cannot tell you how it liberates your thinking and how it removes resentment, anger, frustration and self-pity. These are all terrible human emotions that work like a cancer in us and reduce our lives to nothing.

Many people that read this book will have defined themselves by their job title, their car, their status in a company and the brand of the company they worked for, and some of you will be finding this new road-less-travelled incredibly tough. My hand reaches out to you and all I can say is that those things did not define you then and they do not define you now. As soon as you can let go and see yourself as something far greater than those things your life will transform.

BEING YOU IS ENOUGH

In October 2008 when the news across the world of the collapse of the banking system and the property market was hitting us all hard, I witnessed first-hand many acquaintances that had lived a carefree life with a very high standard of living suddenly have fear on their faces for the first time. For me, it was the second collapse I had seen in ten years, following the e-commerce collapse of 2001.

What I noticed was a fear around me. People had a fear of telling anyone what they were going through. People were staying behind closed doors, unable to go to London shopping with friends as before, unable to meet at expensive restaurants. Suddenly I saw a group of socialites keeping their head down.

One evening I went out with some friends for a drink and we chatted about this and I realized that money can buy you self-esteem and a sense of belonging, but they only last as long as the money doesn't run out. Buying expensive clothes, handbags, watches and cars may give your self-esteem a boost and may enable you to display your value, but that is all. Relying on this alone is not enough.

Being able to go to expensive restaurants and take glamorous holidays where you will meet other glamorous people may give you a sense of belonging, but to what? What I have observed is that that all humans need self-esteem and a sense of belonging. Those with money are in danger of buying it, those who do not rely on money for self-esteem or belonging find they have real friends.

Real friends – what does that mean to you, and are you a real friend to many? Having time to create friendships when we have all been chasing a dream of wealth has not always been possible. I am a victim of that. But what a shame and what a lonely world we have created around ourselves. No wonder children are finding the solution themselves and are living their lives inside Facebook.

Social confidence, a sense of belonging and self-esteem – all these things matter, and within social networks you can nurture and create these, online and offline. In Don Tapscott's book *Wikinomics*, he stressed through his research that the most connected children online were also the most sociable offline.[10]

Social networks are places to create your reputation, a reputation that will become your legacy. Your uniqueness is your opportunity. Your value to others and your contribution is your currency. Treat all those with whom you come into contact with respect and friendship and they will become more than just your social network, they will become your online home and your online place for business.

CHAPTER 4

BUILDING ATTRACTION AND BEING A MAGNET

We HAVE ESTABLISHED that the world is changing and we have a feel for the factors that are creating this change. In his inaugural speech Obama said, 'Greatness must be earned; there are no shortcuts.' The same principle applies to being online.

The confusion surrounding the social media world is huge and every day people are taking a 'leap of faith' into the unknown, with no real feel for what it can achieve for them. There is a feeling that prevails wherever I go and meet people that they know they have to start playing and be part of this new 'thing'. Finding case studies of successes are ten a penny as everyone can quote a moment in their day online where they found the right piece of information or the right person. Woody Allen famously said, 'Ninety per cent of success in life is just showing up. If you're not in the game, you can't win, lucky or not.' The new world is exactly this, you just have to turn up and play.

In this chapter I want to focus your mind on creating relevance and attraction around your personal brand to increase your opportunity for success. While I advocate that you cannot be focused on your own success and that success is the by-product, you do have to create a vibration, I call this an 'emotional vibration' – an atmosphere of who you are and what you can contribute. In other words, create attraction. This comes from the clarity of what you contribute, which we covered in the last chapter, and also it comes from building attraction around you.

DON'T PLAN, JUST PLAY

We have all been taught that 'if you fail to plan then you plan to fail'. This has created a world where we are fearful of doing anything 'off plan'. We are worried that unless we know exactly why we are committing to a task, then we may not hit the bullseye. Tasks dominate our lives, as to-do lists get ever longer. But perhaps there is another way.

One of the most challenging thoughts of the twenty-first century is that planning can perhaps restrict and limit your opportunity for success. I am not advocating that complete chaos rules. However, there is a danger that being targeted with your online networking and utilizing the tools to achieve your 'bullseye' may stop you from having the peripheral vision you need to adapt, compete and achieve success.

In Chapter three I introduced the idea that 'success is the by-product' and that by considering a wider set of motives and by looking at your contribution you can actually achieve success, by accident. We need to look at this more closely.

SERENDIPITY

Serendipity is the effect by which one accidentally discovers something fortunate, especially while looking for something else entirely.

A brilliantly worded explanation on Wikipedia

When you are *not* looking for the answer you will discover what you need to know. Get your head around that thought! One of the toughest ideas I have to teach when explaining the power of social networks and social media is the power of serendipity.

This phrase sounds spiritual and deep, and is hard for task-orientated business people to get their head around. However, we are learning that the random nature of social media is what creates success for all those that take part.

Let's just explore this further but using the offline world. We know that the more people we meet, the more we 'get ourselves out there', and the more we create a brand that others respect and know, the higher the chance of success. My most recent experience of this was when I decided I would like to write this book. One day I arranged to meet with a member of Ecademy, Grant Leboff, a great guy that I admire. I was reminded when we met that he has written a book, it was a very successful book on selling, called *Sales Therapy*.[11] Grant told me that he had been thrilled with his publisher, John Moseley, and that he would introduce me to him.

Two weeks later, John and I met at 10 a.m., my first meeting of the day. I had another meeting planned and then was off to a launch of a new club on Ecademy. John and I hit it off and he said that I should put my thoughts down on two sides of A4 paper and send it to him. From that moment on I knew that my journey to this book had started. The next meeting I had that day was with Claire Richmond, a great lady, also a member of Ecademy, who had created a website for experts to be matched to TV producers, www.findatvexpert.com. I told Claire about my meeting with John and she was very enthusiastic and excited for me and helped me to understand how this will help my brand for TV. I walked from the meeting I had with Claire to the Institute of Directors (IoD) on Pall Mall, to join the launch party that was taking place for the new club on Ecademy. The club was called The Purple Cow Club. Sitting listening to its leader, Sue Richardson, I heard that the plan for the club was to help rising stars that are writing books, providing them with all the collaborative needs to make them successful. Sitting opposite me was a lovely gentleman who had just completed his book and he suggested that it would help me to have some academic support for mine. You got it. The next meeting I had was with a programme director from the University of Buckingham, Nigel Adams, who offered to help me with researchers.[12] Serendipity at work and at play!

The point here is that I had arranged these meetings at random. Some had been arranged months previously. I had no idea that these meetings would have so much meaning to me. My fortune was due to my wide, random network that came to my support at the point when I needed it. My intention for the meetings was to help those I met, to guide them in the world of social media. The value I received I feel outweighed the value I gave them in the end.

The tremendous aspect of social media is the wide, random reach that each of us can achieve from our home, talking globally to people from many walks of life. We are broadening our horizons, but at the same time, the wider it becomes the more time it saves and the more sense it makes!

In writing this section of the book I decided to reach out to the community on Ecademy and ask them for their thoughts. I wrote the following blog at 1.37 p.m. on 10 February 2009:

Please help me explain 'serendipity' and how social media accelerates its occurrence.

When I checked on 12 February at 11.05 a.m. I had 95 comments from members and over 1,700 views of my blog.[13] One member, Mary D. Moore, said, 'What I had accomplished in two years of building my business would have been an accomplishment in ten years had it not been for the social media and serendipity.'

Here are a couple more extracts that I think will be helpful.

From Nigel Biggs:[14]

Serendipity has always happened but it has not been so visible or so traceable before the arrival of global, internet-based networks. In the 'old days' our marketing was always broadcast, we had no control or evidence of forwarded links via leaflets,word of mouth, etc. (but they did happen) and then somehow we get a call from a completely unexpected source.

Today those forwardings, recommendations, etc. are online in a more visible way. So your 'vibrations' (just like ripples in a lake when a stone is dropped in) are more tangible. Twitter is more about 'short-wave' vibrations that have a limited life. 'Long-wave' vibrations (e-mails, blogs, etc.) have a longer life and travel further and give more opportunity to provide awareness and reaction in really hidden and unexpected corners of the world.

From Doug Holman:[15]

With the advent of social media, examples [of serendipity] 'just happen' all the time. Just this morning I received an invitation to read and comment on a blog from an Ecademist in New Zealand who only recently connected using the contact request feature. Although the blog was nothing whatsoever to do with business, I was sufficiently intrigued to click on the author's profile button and lo and behold the following text leapt off the screen: 'If you know of anyone who has great downloadable business/training products get in touch with me urgently!' Needless to say, I managed to think of someone!

For what it's worth, I believe it all boils down to someone's sense of purpose. Those – possibly a majority – who have not yet figured out their 'mission' do not seem to experience these events as often, so perhaps it's more difficult for them to appreciate how serendipity works. Those who are focused, persisting in spite of life's distractions, usually find it easier. Of course, this doesn't make them superior, just different, like the maverick animals on the aptly named Serengeti that graze separately. Darwin recognized that mavericks are an essential part of natural selection, helping species survive the occasional disaster that wipes out the rest of the herd.

What if social media acts as a catalyst, grazed on by all, not just mavericks? What if it accelerates the occurrence of serendipity only in those with a purpose?

Wouldn't that motivate others to find and pursue a purpose, to the benefit of all?

Awesome comments from two random connections. Across the internet on all of the social networks people are finding the answers, the people and the ideas that they did not know they needed when they woke up that morning. Through the random searching of links, people are being serendipitously connected. The wonderful thing is that neither party targeted one another, but as a result of their online 'collision' a force was created that took them in a direction that they needed.

Like being a scholar for life, people who see the internet as a constant learning place are spotting opportunities and inspiring thoughts at a speed that we can only wonder at and try to be part of. Coming to terms with the thought that every connection, every click has a cause and effect is quite a shift in thinking.

So how can you ensure that your contribution, your unique opportunity to help someone at that specific moment in time happens? The answer is having a large network and contributing actively across the internet – on social media sites and within social networks – and, critically, by understanding what thoughts you want to influence and what your song is. As Doug Holman says, it begins with understanding your purpose, or as I like to put it, knowing what song you are singing.

SINGING YOUR SONG

As a child I remember witnessing that one of my older relatives had so much potential, so much to contribute, so much they could have achieved, but that they had never actually sung their song. What is your song? Defining your song is like finding an answer to why you were born. Every person that has been placed on earth has a unique contribution to make. Finding purpose in your 'being' is not about having a mid-life crisis, it is not about you! Once you find your song you realize it is about who hears you, not about the fact that you are singing it.

Putting all the things that make up you into a melting pot and seeing what words emerge will help you to make sense of your life and your contribution. When I was a child I thought that everyone has to sing their song while on earth and how terribly, terribly sad it would be if they died with their song still in their heart. Knowing the song you want to sing is the first step to building attraction and creating the influence you want to have within the online world. I have created, in collaboration with thousands of people, the type of place where this can be achieved. Social media allows your song to be sung loud and clear, and you don't even have to be performing it when it is heard!

Open a Word document and throw out the answers that you think of under these headings:

- My talents – what makes my heart beat faster?
- My education – what do I feel was relevant?
- My job experiences – what did I do that provided satisfaction?
- My skills – why did someone pay me for my skills?
- My pains – what did I learn through adversity?
- My joys – what made me happiest?
- My weaknesses – what do I accept I cannot do?
- My strengths – what do I do that is easy for me?
- My contribution – what do I do that solves problems?
- My song – if I sang aloud what would it be about?

JOINING THE DOTS

I have been in awe of Steve Jobs (co-founder of Apple) for over twenty years. His ability to take risks, to do things differently, to change business and to contribute to people has been a constant amazement to me; he is one of my heroes. A year ago I was sent a link to his speech at Stamford University, you can find it on YouTube and I appeal to you to listen to it.[16] I have extracted a section of his speech below, it is incredible and I hope gives you faith in my message.

> It was impossible to connect the dots looking forward when I was in college, but it was very, very clear looking backwards ten years later. Again, you can't connect the dots looking forward, you can only connect them looking backwards, so you have to trust in something, your gut, destiny, life, karma, whatever, because believing that the dots will connect down the road will give you the confidence to follow your heart, even when it leads you off the well-worn path, and that will make all the difference.
>
> Steve Jobs, Stamford University
> Commencement Speech, 2005

The message here is make lots of dots in your life and then look at the dots and you will see what you have created. I love the analogy of the dots, as I see these as links that you create inside social networks and across the social media platforms. You cannot always see the sense of them, you cannot always get an instant result, but over time they make sense to you when that random person, event or opportunity comes your way. You can trace it back to that chance moment, that contribution you made somewhere, which led that person to you.

WHAT IS IN YOUR HEART WILL DETERMINE YOUR SUCCESS

If I could have a pound for every time I have been told that I am too emotional then I would be able to feed all the hungry in this world. When I went into business at nineteen I was under the impression that emotion was supposed to be left at the door. I now know and I am proud to shout out that what is in your heart will determine your success. What is in your brain is the intelligence you need to make the difference that your heart wants you to make.

Seven years ago I wrote my first business speech. It was for BT and its title was 'Connecting your heart to your head'. There I was, on stage as an adult, as a business person, in a 'proper' company and I had permission to share my emotion about business. The reception I received after my talk and the ongoing business and friendships I have had since that day have inspired me to continue with my firm belief that emotion is part of business. I have Jane Swift, a good friend and a brilliant businesswoman, to thank for that.

Separating your emotional intention from your business life is a twentieth-century myth. Business is about people and people are about emotions. They make emotional decisions. When anyone buys anything it is to alleviate some form of emotional need. Twentieth-century business models were about pushing the customer away from the business, automating, separating and looking for cost-saving ways of serving their needs. Yet how did companies know what their consumers needs were? Large organizations that have adopted this approach have become so separated from the customer that they have no idea of their needs, they just know what they want to sell to them. But what happens when the customer stops buying or when their needs change?

When you start to communicate your message, when you begin to sing your song, you will hear that the tune has emotion, has a beat. By appealing to the heart of the customers you will create more attraction than you ever imagined possible. In order to do this you must stop thinking about you and start thinking about the needs of your customer, in fact of everyone that you come into contact with. Connect your heart to your head and understand what problems you are solving for people you come into contact with, not what you are selling.

DO YOU SELL OR DO YOU SUPPLY?

In an ideal world you would create enough attraction around you that you would never have to sell. People would just ask if they can buy from you. Traditional sales techniques have centered around 'trapping' your customer through mind games – using open questions not closed ones, selling features and benefits. Twenty-first-century business models are centered around creating an attraction around you that encourages your audience to want to buy from you, built on trust, caring, sharing, collaboration and an understanding that you have their best intentions at the core of your thoughts.

I remember in the 1980s when I worked for a UK-based computer distributor, we suddenly came under attack from the USA. American distributors entered the UK market and with greater buying power they were able to undercut our prices. At the time we had 5,000 PC dealers on our books and we had a loyal following of customers who trusted us. Our sole aim was to be the first place they called when they needed a laserprinter for their end-user.

We could not compete on price with the US companies,

we had to find something else. We opted for relationships. We knew that if customers saw that we cared about their business more than our own that we would have a chance of maintaining our position in the market.

I had a team of eighty telesales people and five product managers who looked after the 2,000 product lines. We trained the salespeople to really understand the life of a computer dealer, how tough it could be dealing with the end-user and all the expectations of that person. As a distributor we were removed from the stress of the end-user, but it didn't mean we couldn't empathize with the life of the buyer who was trying to keep their customer happy. Satisfying their needs became more important than selling our stock. Their needs were our needs.

The computer industry at that time was growing at hyper-speed and the demand was unbelievable. Stock maintenance was a regular problem, with manufacturers finding it hard to satisfy the demands of the end-user. We created a routine every day in our business to ensure that whatever happened, the dealer would be OK. He/she would be able to supply their end-user. Every morning we would run a report on our stock, anything that was out of stock our product manager would call our competitors and find out if they had it. A list of where the stock was held within the UK was given to all the salespeople. If any dealer called for a product that we didn't have stock of they were able to apologize and tell them who did have the stock. We collaborated with our competitors to ensure that the wheels kept turning for our dealers. As a result we were loved, respected and were always the first point of call.

The lesson here is not about finding ways to sell your products, it is about sending out a 'feeling' into the world that tells people who you care about, what your contribution is and that you have a network that satisfies those needs and if you cannot fill it, you know someone who can. This is attraction.

BUILDING YOUR ATTRACTION

The more active I am online, the more I notice that links in the online world create a web of influence around an individual, and the emotional vibrations they send out creates an attraction. The vibrations are like a magnet, drawing people, opportunities and knowledge towards them.

Everything on the internet is linked. Links found within websites take you off in random directions and enable you to bump into new people and new pieces of information. The more links there are about you, the greater your visibility on the internet.

When e-commerce began in the mid-1990s many businesses set up an online store. Most websites were equivalent to having a shed down a five-mile track that no one could see. People became obsessed with being found on Google. The holy grail was knowing that Google would find *your* website when the person searching matched the words that you had put into the search engines. The search engine optimization (SEO) world exploded and this became one of the key investments businesses had to make 'to be found'.

FIND ME

Social media is becoming a 'be found' engine. But being found is no longer about someone searching for you, it is about random thoughts and random conversations that somehow lead the person with the need to the person who can solve it.

Google is still the number one place to be found and access knowledge and information. However, being found is not necessarily just about taking someone to your website by optimizing your website through the tools you can use or by purchasing adverts on Google. It is also about attracting someone to you, as the knowledge provider or the person who has the connections to the people with the knowledge. You cannot be found unless you are contributing content in some shape or form. When you search now on Google it is the content and people on social media sites such as YouTube, Flickr, Twitter, Ecademy, LinkedIn, Facebook and Wikipedia, to name a handful, that come up on the first page. Being found inside the social media world is now the best way of being found.

A critical mistake people often make is that while you may be easy to find via Google, how easy is it to connect with you, the holder of the knowledge they want to access? Do you still protect yourself, just like you asked your switchboard to protect you in the corporate world? If you do, then you are still hanging on to control, assuming that people might 'waste your time', that people might not be useful to you. If you are not ready to make a change then please start rereading this book from the beginning! Remember, it is up to you to contribute to others, it is not their job to contribute to you.

The more visibility you have inside social media the more opportunities will come your way, and you *will* be found. How often you are found is a result of your attraction and that is a reflection of your knowledge contribution and network size. If you have a small network inside LinkedIn, Ecademy or Twitter that tells the world that you do not want to help, that being found makes no sense to you, I am afraid to say it tells the world that you are a taker because if your network is small, what are you doing to help others? If many people follow you, if your networks are large, there must be a reason, not least will be the fact that you are sharing and connecting a great deal. (Of course Twitter celebrities are the exception!)

When someone searches for information online it begins a random path of links to information and people that they had not originally known they needed. These links take the surfer deeper and deeper into the subject, hopefully deepening the intensity of the search and taking them closer to the source of the knowledge they need. When acting in this random and embracing way it allows new information and new people into their network and their knowledge bank. This is the way to find new opportunities and inspire new thoughts.

When I help my children with their homework we have an idea of the information we want to retrieve and if we stay focused we can deliver an essay on a period of history or geography subject that fulfils the promises of that homework. However, when we allow ourselves the time to open our minds and stretch our boundaries, we create a broader, more researched view of the subject, delivering a far more over-whelming result. What we achieve by allowing more information in, is context and an understanding of why, how and who. This provides a greater depth of meaning to our knowledge.

The other day I was searching for information on Seth Godin, as I wanted to read what other people had said about his book, *The Dip*. When I googled it, I came across a blog written by a man called Parke Ladd.[17] He had some notes about his thoughts on *The Dip*. They were very helpful. I didn't finish searching and surfing at this point. I noticed on his blog site a great quote by Steve Jobs. I liked it and it made me have an understanding of how Parke Ladd was feeling at this moment in time. I also noticed that rather than just broadcast this knowledge to me in his blog, he was also offering me an opportunity to have a dialogue with him via his Twitter page. Inspired by his use of the Steve Jobs quote, I decided to follow Parke on Twitter. Now Parke has another follower and the two of us are connected. Within a day, Parke linked back to me and followed me on Twitter. We have now exchanged a few words and I know that I can keep up to date with him and he with me. It will be interesting where this serendipitous moment takes the two of us, but already here I am talking about him and providing a link to his blog in this book. What was the attraction to Parke? How did the intention he shared through his blog attract me to be connected to him? It is an important point to consider.

In contrast to this, I was advised that Mark Earls would be a great guy to know and meet.[18] Mark wrote a book called *Herd* and I was interested to connect with him. I googled his name and found many links to his resources. I could read all about him, I could see he was a LinkedIn user, had a Facebook profile and also ran his own blogs. I was attracted to his knowledge, but I could not connect with him. That is where my journey with Mark ended. Unlike Parke Ladd, it was not easy to connect and go from stranger to 'friend'.

As discussed in Chapter three, social media sites provide many experiences and they all stem from the origins of the intention that the sites have. I mentioned that Mark Earls had a profile on LinkedIn, and also Facebook, so you must be wondering why I could not connect with him, yet I could connect with Parke through Twitter. The reason is simply that Twitter and Ecademy allow random connections, LinkedIn does not. You can only connect with a new person via an introduction.

Facebook has its origins in students and the younger generation. Cautious of paedophiles, it prevented strangers being able to see your photos and your network. I can understand this and I embrace it, my children are devoted users of Facebook. From a business point of view I guess I see a potential dilemma for people who do embrace the random.

Social media is about being easy to connect with, so you need to use multiple places to build your visibility and to ensure you are found. Setting aside the exceptional reason for Facebook protecting their members, creating barriers to protect yourself is a dangerous game to play. Managing your life by exception and fearing the odd time-waster will limit your success. You are distributing brand YOU and it is essential that you fear nothing and that you are willing to allow anyone into your online world. To be a magnet within the online world you have to know your intention and your contribution and then be everywhere.

The danger in staying in the old values that many of us embraced while working in institutions and hierarchies is that we remain closed, selective and controlling when we network, when the world is becoming open, random and supportive.

To complete this thought consider this: I said that Google helps you find knowledge and that Twitter helps you connect with the people that have the knowledge. Which is more powerful?

FINDING YOUR VALUE IN OTHERS

The more you publish information, share connections and provide thoughts, the more you will discover your value and your intention. I have found that by understanding others I have gained a greater understanding of myself. The questions they ask, the feedback I receive, the success or the failures I have had all provide me with the knowledge I need about myself to understand my value and my weaknesses. The feedback you get from those that 'bump' into you randomly will enable you to see your value far more clearly than you will ever understand if you look inwards at yourself.

Your value is based only on the value others place on you. Think about this. I could tell you that a beautiful painting I did when I was ten is worth £1,000. I could say this until I was blue in the face and you may disagree. However, imagine a few people were interested in it and that people started to talk about it. Some people showed others a copy of it. Suddenly what I was saying would be true but not because I said it, but because others could also see the value and wanted to share that with their friends. This is true of you, you need to have the links and the visibility, but critically, others will decide if they are attracted to you and that you are valuable to know.

Your value is based on what people say about you when you are not there and what attraction you have created around you by your words, actions and thoughts. If you stay small, have few people talking about you and you have little visibility, your value will be less. Worse still, you could be utterly brilliant but too hard to find. What a terrible waste that is.

On 13 February 2009 I went back to my blog and I had been left this quote. 'Everyone and everything will find you, if you are findable.' Thank you Michael Pokocky.[19]

CREATING ATTRACTION

I have created a Ten-point Action Plan to help you create attraction, which summarizes what I have stated in this chapter.

1. Understand your expertise

The hardest part about creating your value online is having an understanding of what your expertise is. At a talk I gave recently, I had sixty people in the room and I asked everyone to put their hand up if they believed they were an expert in their area of knowledge and business. Almost the whole room put their hand up. I then asked them to tell me what they were an expert in and there was silence, followed by a few garbled, lengthy replies that were quite embarrassing. There were two people in the room that said they were experts in helping people discover their expertise. Wow! Talk about a room full of opportunity for them. In fact, joking apart, this was quite serious. In a room of sixty professionals, each person earning above average income, each having held good jobs in the corporate world, no one could really explain their expertise.

An expert is a person with extensive knowledge or ability in a particular area. The key is knowledge. Many people think they are an expert, but do they know what knowledge they can share?

You must create a vibration of intent, a feeling about you, an atmosphere of trust, a desire to contact you when someone needs an answer to a problem that only you can answer. You want to be that person that people turn to. You need to be knowledgeable.

At the same talk there was a gentleman, James McBrearty, in the room who had 'Tax Specialist' on his badge.[20] He was a quiet man, standing on the periphery of the room, observing everyone, clearly a thinker and a good man. During Thomas's speech Thomas pointed James out and asked him what he did.

James: I help people with their tax.
Thomas: What type of people?

James: Small businesses.
Thomas: How small?
James: With a turnover of less than £50,000.
Thomas: In what geography?
James: Surrey.
Thomas: Do you help with corporate or personal tax?
James: Personal.

James has a crystal-clear intention – to reduce the tax burden on the small-business owner.

The more precise you are about your expertise the more opportunities everyone can pass to you, the more clarity you have about your intention and the greater the amount of content and knowledge you can share with others.

Until you know what your contribution is, what you really want to achieve for others, what your song is, it is very hard to create attraction. Think about your wider purpose and what gives you a buzz when you are helping a client, then focus on delivering this message and sharing this knowledge. James knows and when he talks about it everyone in the room could tell he really meant it and suddenly tax was not boring! When James is sharing this online in blogs and inside groups he will then build attraction.

2. Build a reputation, build a brand

Your reputation and your face is your brand. What people say about you will determine your success.

In 2005 I was asked to talk about network value at a conference in Bali. It is strange, but I had to think hard about this, I had to find a simple explanation for what it means to have 'network value'. How do you measure the value in your network? It came to me, and it is simple.

Your network value is based on what people say about you

when you are not there. You can only create value in your network of contacts if they trust you, understand you and know you can contribute a lot when someone they refer to you needs help. Create a reputation that others respect and are happy to be associated with. Give them something clear, emotional and powerful so that they know who you are and when and why they should recommend you or ask you for help. Your reputation is so important to you, it is the most critical asset you have, yet it is so easily lost. It is what you leave behind when you die. Nurture it, build it and care for it.

I have also learnt from the last eleven years that your photo, in effect your face, is also your brand. It creates a feeling, an instant impression, and you should spend time making sure you are happy with it. Use a good picture of yourself and use the same one on all online networks you are in. Consistency is vital.

Your name is also your brand – more so than your company name, as it is you that is creating the content, you that is passing on connections, you that is helping others. Don't hide behind a company name or an online avatar. Be proud of yourself and make your name your brand. One further thought: I have registered my children's names on Twitter. I wanted to make sure that their name becomes a brand for them one day. Once your name has been taken, it is gone.

3. Be positive

Over the years I have seen many people destroy their brands by being negative, cruel and angry. If you find yourself in this state, stay away from the keyboard. Remember, the online links can remain forever and become your legacy. Sadly, over the eleven years of building Ecademy we have lost some members as they have died. We have been asked by many of the relatives of these people to keep their profile up, their links, their testimonials, their blog, as this is who they were while they were alive. This is a thought for us all and should make us consider our legacy. Your online profile is immortal.

I was once told about 'drains' and 'radiators'. I googled the terms recently and found that they were first used by Tim Melville Ross, who was director general of the Institute of Directors. I learnt this thanks to Roger Knight[21] on his Happy and Prosperous blog[22], which quoted Tim Melville Ross as follows:

> Over the years I learnt there are two types of people – the 'radiators' and the 'drains'. Radiators give them-selves with enthusiasm to any project, whereas drains consume energy with negativity and moaning. Surround yourself with the former and you will succeed. Of course you have to be a radiator yourself.

I have always loved this quote, it provides so many meanings. 'Radiators' are people that you love to be close to, they warm you, when you step away you miss them, they provide comfort and make you feel great. 'Drains' on the other hand, drain you, like a drain in the ground, you feel like you want to fall down, they make you feel low and take away your energy. As Roger says in his blog, drains 'moan about things, take the pessimistic point of view, rubbish other people's ideas', whereas radiators 'are upbeat, enthusiastic, encouraging, positive and optimistic, radiating energy and inspirational'. I wonder which type of person you want to be known as?

4. Reputation by association

So, looking at the idea of being a 'radiator' or a 'drain', which one are you and, critically, who are you associated with? The online world can be like the school playground. Be careful of the bullies who attract you towards them and try to place you in their 'gang'. This sounds totally ridiculous in an adult world but believe me, this goes on. If you are in clubs, groups and networks that are full of negative, angry people, you will be associated with them.

At a training event recently I was asked what do I do when I get linked to someone who I feel it is not good to be associated with. My advice is think about who you 'hang out' with and whatever you do, don't get dragged down to their level. The best you can do is make sure you stay away from people who you instinctively feel may damage your reputation.

There is a big difference between visibility and credibility. I know many people who have a very visible brand, but zero credibility; the balance is critical. Be aware of this at all times.

In 2007 I was introduced to the concept created by Ivan Misner, the founder of the business referral network, BNI (Business Network International).[23] In 2008 Ivan wrote an excellent blog that I highly recommend called the 'VCP Process®Æ'[24]. In this blog Ivan talks about visibility and credibility leading to profitable relationships. CNN call him the 'father of modern networking'. He is a phenomenal man with the greatest values and a business that reflects his understanding of 'Giver's Gain', the motto of BNI.

Ivan explains that the first part of any business relationship is visibility, people becoming aware that you exist; the second is credibility, when you build trust and confidence. The danger of being associated with 'the wrong' people is that you will find it tough to move to the second part of the relationship – credibility – if trust and worthiness do not come across. These are factors that many will link to the people you 'hang out with'. There is much we can learn from Ivan's offline network (which hosts over 5,400 breakfasts a week across the world) that we can apply to the online world; they mirror one another in so many ways.

5. Love what you do

If you want others to advocate you and to believe in you then you must show that you love what you do. If you don't feel this way, then you are doing the wrong thing. No one will connect you to a person in need unless they trust that you will passionately care about the end result.

Looking back at 'drains and radiators', the same applies to loving what you do. If you moan and whine about how tired you are, about difficult clients, about not enjoying your work, it will not help you achieve successful financial results. In fact, I will go as far as saying you have to make a change in your life if you feel that way. You have one life and in that life you should be a happy song, a bright light, a cheerful presence. You can only be this if you are either a brilliant actor or if you genuinely love what you do.

This is why I say that my focus is to increase the emotional and financial wealth of business owners. Without emotional wealth and happiness it is tough for money to flow. So learn to love what you do or do something different. Your network is there to support you, as I am sure you will be supporting them. Ask those around you what makes you shine, what they notice you are happiest doing, ask them what they feel you contribute and then build on that.

I mentioned that I went to Bali in 2005 to give a talk. I was invited to do this by Roger Hamilton, a man I have known for over twelve years.[25] Roger is a 'wealth guru'. He is an incredibly clever man with a great heart and a busy mind. Roger dedicates his life to entrepreneurs and wants to help them find their 'flow' and make millions from doing this. He also wants those people who make money to give back and help others, creating 'World Wide Wealth'.[26]

I have learnt many things through my association with Roger, my favourite is about imagining yourself as a candle. Like a candle, you have a flame and you have wax. The flame part of you is when you are loving what you do, when you are a bright light, shining and warm. When you are working 'in your flame' you are full of energy, you can light a million other candles without losing energy, you are 'on fire'. You will know when you are 'in your flame' as you are instinctively working and contributing. Many people when they start their business or begin a new job are 'in the flame' and it shows. They are happy, healthy and highly attractive to be associated with and to know.

The wax element is the part that drags you down, that reduces in value, makes you feel tired, that can actually drown out the flame and in time makes you so negative and tired that you stop lighting other candles and lighting the world around you. You know when you are like this as you feel tired at the end of your day, you are performing outside of your skill set and life feels tough.

To create attraction you need to find a way of being 'in your flame' as often as possible, to love what you are doing and compartmentalize the areas of your life that are your 'wax'. None of us can avoid having wax, this is the routine part of your life that just has to be done, but be aware of those tasks and avoid doing them when you need to be 'on fire', when you are creating attraction.

Being in a network has taught me that one person's flame is another person's wax, and one person's wax is another person's flame. I might love public speaking and writing blogs and feel energized by these activities; however, give me bookkeeping and I would fade away. My flame is to teach and share, not to do administration tasks. Thomas's flame is meeting, collecting and connecting people. We learnt early in building Ecademy to empathize with one another in our company and ensure that we knew what each of us loved doing and what each of us hated and we found ways of helping one another stay in our flame as much as possible. Once we applied this, our business grew. People we come into contact with see us at our best, happy and loving what we do.

It is worth spending time thinking about what makes you feel like you are a flame and what is taking you into your wax. When you feel that tremendous warmth and tingle up your spine and you know that you are on fire and contributing at your best, write it down, capture it, because that is what you love doing. This is what you should write about, leverage and find ways of making money out of. This is what you love to be and do.

Likewise, when you discover your wax, those things you dislike doing, try to find people in your network that love those tasks and just ask them what they would charge to do them for you. This is how businesses are forming now, sharing tasks and helping one another stay in our flame.

6. Know what you stand for

I once heard that 'if you stand for nothing, then you will fall for everything'. I believe it was Hermann Hesse who said this.[27] It is important to have standards, values and beliefs that represent you, outside of purely commercial interests.

Online you will have moments when you want to take part in discussions and debates. What you say will provide the reader with an experience of your values. If you don't stand for something and go through life caring only about your own experiences, then you will appear one-dimensional and shallow. Online there are many causes, clubs and groups that will enjoy you participating. When you do this, make sure that you do this with a positive attitude and that the footprint you leave reflects your wider values. Doing this will attract people that would normally not be within your area of expertise or interests, this is how you broaden your appeal.

7. Relationships first, commerce second

Thomas first used this phrase over ten years ago, in the 1990s. Like many phrases it can take time to understand the full impact of living this way. I have learned so much from watching Thomas and listening to his 'followers' and his critics. Thomas embraces anyone who wants to know him, he is awesome with his generosity and countless times he has been sent messages saying he has 'changed lives'.

When I asked Thomas to explain what he loves about meeting people and how he helps them, this is what he said to me: 'I focus on knowing the whole person, and I wait until people are ready to tell me their personal and private things, in other words, until they are ready to share their whole self. It is through sharing this over time that I learn to know how, where and if I can help someone or work with them, either as a buyer or a supplier. I never assume this level of communication and trust; I wait for the right time to emerge. You don't have to push a relationship, they happen when they are ready.'

I then remember one of the stories that first inspired me to create Ecademy, along with the two books I read. In 1998 Thomas told me about a Microsoft project that was created to look at 'community'. They created a website named after a street in Seattle. They leaflet-dropped the neighbourhood and requested that people joined the site and added their name and their occupation and anything else they were willing to share.

The results of the 'test' were amazing. People who had never physically met in the street were talking online and even helping one another, trading with one another and becoming friends. People do want friendship and they do want to know you, but many have forgotten how to do this. The world is becoming so isolated. Eighty-four per cent of our members are working from home. Friendship is such a gift and it is the best way to build trust and really understand someone's values and intention.

In a recent visit to a group of members I met a very special person. She told me that she loved Ecademy and she explained to me what work she did. I asked her what her reason for working was and what she told me inspired me so much to get to know her more, to help her and to advocate her.

She told me that she had an arranged marriage and that she loved her husband. They had moved from India and she now had a young daughter. A year ago she had been put under pressure by her husband and mother-in-law to send her daughter, aged five, back to India for her schooling. This would separate her from her daughter, meaning that she would see her only in the school holidays. The thought devastated her. So she committed to her husband that she would work and bring enough income in to educate her daughter in the country that they were now living in. It would take a cold heart not to be moved by that. Now I want to know who she needs to meet and what information will help her. Now I want to advocate her. Now I want her to be successful.

Social media is so-called for a reason. While amazing business can be created through this 'media' you cannot treat it in the same way as you treated your marketing plans in the past. The most damaging thing you can do is to broadcast a message to a network that is sales related. The online community is not afraid to ignore you if you break some basic ethics. The internet is absolutely not a broadcast medium, it is a conversation medium. Remember, 'relationship first, commerce second'. This most applies when you are sending a message and when you have moved beyond communicating one-to-many. I think the biggest complaint that I see on many sites is when someone violates the connection they have made and been given as a measure of trust, by broadcasting to them.

Finally, as Thomas says, 'Don't try to manipulate relationships with commerce in mind, you will fail.'

8. Be random

When we started Ecademy it was interesting to compare the way Thomas networked with the way I did. Thomas was able to handle and encourage a very wide network embracing the random. I, on the other hand, went for depth. I wanted to honour everyone and build a relationship. I felt the need to reply personally, with time and patience to every message. So in a sense I was a conversationalist and Thomas was a communicator.

We had some great arguments about this. I now know Thomas was right and he now knows that I am right. This is because there is no right or wrong, there are just different ways of networking. Instinctively you will know when you read this which approach you favour. I hear everyone's view on this and all I can do is explain the benefits of both. I will do this in a later chapter, on page 126 – mile wide and mile deep networking.

One of the areas that intrigues me is why people would not welcome new contacts into their life, judging quality and quantity in a split second. Your brand will grow the more people that know you exist. The new world is different and you are now 'out there' in the ether, with your name being distributed in random, unstructured, uncontrollable ways. This will bring with it some people who 'bump' into you that you may not have been targeting. This is not a list of prospects that you can conduct a telesales campaign on, these are just 'people'. Last year I had a rewarding trip with Thomas to meet members in Slovenia. A wonderful lady, Andreja Lajh, runs the Ecademy Slovenia Club.[28] Andreja held a networking weekend and members from over ten European countries came to meet up. The stories of business that was happening between each of them due to 'random bumps' were fantastic.

Thomas and I had many one-to-one meetings with members. One of them sticks in my mind very strongly, because I think I was in a wicked mood! A beautiful, vibrant lady was sitting opposite me. She was enthusiastically thanking Ecademy for some changes it had made to her business life and the people she had met. Her husband came along out of curiosity and was sitting opposite us with his arms crossed and sitting well back in his chair observing us. In time he moved forwards and looked me in the eye and said, 'This social networking thing, I guess I should start doing this?' I said that it would be a good idea. He then asked, 'How do I find only the quality people?'

Well there you have it, the problem that faces so many people when they consider this enormous, random world. At this point I became a little naughty with this unsuspecting man. I leant forwards and said, 'I understand your dilemma, because I can tell you are a quality person and therefore you only want to deal with "quality people".' He looked relieved and smiled warmly. I then asked him to go home that night and write down all the things that make up a 'quality person'. He wrote this down neatly in his notebook. I asked him to bring that list back to us and I would pass it to my coders, the team who write the code for the website, and ask them to write some code into his profile that would filter only the quality people to him. As he was writing this down, his writing became slower and he looked up and said, 'You can't do that can you?' To which I answered, 'I am afraid we can't, and nor can you.'

Really, the only filter on quality is the intentions of the people around us, their values and the way they treat others. You cannot know this until you get to know them, so, welcome others with open arms.

All 'quality networks' have a way of blocking or un-following people. Many networks will enable you to stop unwanted people from being able to contact you so that you can protect yourself from anyone who is broadcasting or spamming you. However, be very careful of blocking or pre-judging people. Many people block out the large networkers, the hypernetworkers, because they feel they are 'gaming' the system. In time, we will all see that those people are the ones who hold the value for the rest of us.

Growing a large, random network is precisely what you need to do, not only to be visible, but also to be able to communicate with a lot of people when you need help, information or the perfect contact to fulfil a need. Critically, having a large network also reflects that you embrace everyone and is an indicator of your attraction and your willingness to help.

I mentioned James McBrearty earlier. I thought I would share something he told me that he achieved through a chance random encounter.

I was looking at the Ecademy homepage back in October last year and spotted an unusual picture in the people online. Most of them were standard business photos, but this one was in black and white and he was wearing a baseball cap! I clicked on it and found an interesting profile, so sent off a standard connection request, which came back with a message in response. We met up to discuss business and as a result he was able to refer one of his friends to us and we completed their tax return in January this year.

9. A favour a day

It is very difficult for anyone to understand how you could possibly support others when you need to work so hard to care for yourself and your family. Whenever I discuss this aspect of social networking with new people they struggle with it. They say that they have enough friends and family around them who need their help and they simply don't have enough time to give any more.

Being supportive means supporting others when they need it. It doesn't mean you have to offer counselling, coaching and advice to everyone you meet, it simply means spending moments in your day allowing yourself to look up and see the world around you and finding a moment to help someone.

On my profile I have the expression 'a favour a day'. This is my personal mantra. Wikipedia's definition of mantra is:[29]

> Mantras can be interpreted to be effective as vibration, or more simply as sound, which may include verbal repetition, in the form of chanting, or internal mental repetition.

This is exactly what 'a favour a day' is for me. Something that has become so deep within my soul that I don't have to consciously think about it any more, it is just my daily vibration. If you look outwards at the world it is very easy to achieve this, so easy it is not a task, it is a pleasure.

Look out for blogs that you can comment on, groups that are discussing something that you can contribute to and people that you can welcome. This is no different to you answering a stranger's request for directions in the street or holding the door open for someone. It takes awareness, it takes a good person, but when you do 'a favour a day', life will feel good.

Several years ago I heard the following story on the radio. I love this so much that I often tell it in training and talks.

There is a man called Captain Charles Plumb, who was a US Navy Pilot.[30] He completed seventy-five missions and then was shot down by a surface-to-air missile. He ejected from the plane and parachuted into enemy hands where he spent the next six years in a Vietnamese prison. He survived.

Many years later he was sitting with his wife in a restaurant and a man who was sitting several tables away from him walked over and introduced himself by saying that he knew who Captain Plumb was and the fact that he had flown a Kitty Hawk and was shot down.

Astonished, Captain Plumb asked him how he knew this information and the man replied, 'I packed your parachute.' The thrill of meeting this man overwhelmed Captain Plumb, as he had saved his life.

That night Captain Plumb lay in bed wondering how he had treated the man, who was a sailor; it worried him. How many hours did he spend on that long, wooden table in the bowels of that ship weaving the shrouds and folding the silks of those chutes? I couldn't have cared less . . . until one day my parachute saved my life.

Captain Plumb now gives talks on this, asking his audience to consider all the people in their lives who are packing their parachute. He also asks, 'Who looks to you for strength in times of need?'

10. Let go

I have explained throughout this book that an open attitude to people is critical. Twentieth-century values encouraged a closed, secretive and controlling set of attitudes; a need to be in control of your day, your spam, your connections, your mailing lists, who gets through to you on the switchboard and who you give your mobile phone number to. It was about a need to hide your intellectual property, a closed view of who is 'allowed' to contact you. These values will hold you back in the twenty-first century, there is no place for them now.

Being an open person is critical to your success. Sharing your ideas, collaborating with your 'competitors' and being open to new things will provide you with all the opportunities, support and funding you need. Once you let go of your fears, you will see over and over again why this makes sense.

I recently did a training course for fifteen people, introducing them to the concepts that you are reading in this book. I love doing this as my aim is always to take people from one place and lead them gently into a new way of thinking. It often takes a paradigm shift, a total change in a way of thinking to make this happen.

At the start of the training I met everyone, greeted them as they came in and started to get a 'feeling' about them. One of the delegates was a sophisticated man, clearly a business-man, dressed in a suit. He was definitely an observer. I could detect that he was very unsure as to why he had booked on the course. However, he was a business coach, and I guess felt that he needed to embrace something that his clients were asking him to help them with. His body language was very off-putting. I knew I had a tough one to crack!

Of course, he sat away from us when everyone was getting their coffee and he chose a seat in the room to listen from that was away from my comfort zone. He was there on his own terms and I was not going to get in the way.

We had a brilliant time, all of us; the room was filled with open minds, lapping it up. One gentleman at the beginning expressed that his goal for being in the room was to understand the 'success factors' for social networking. I asked him if I could save that until we wrapped up and asked everyone in the room to contribute. He was comfortable with this.

At the end of the training, we went back to the flip chart and I wrote 'Success factors' on the paper. Contributions flowed from everyone – 'be random', be open', 'help others', 'build your brand', etc. and then, a quiet voice spoke, my nemesis. He had listened intently, he had written his notes, he had remained unemotional throughout and this is what he said: 'Let go.'

If I could have bottled that moment in my life I would have. It is a moment I shall cherish. For that man, I had achieved a paradigm shift. This was not only going to mean he would utilize social networks, and do it well, it also meant that in life he was going to 'let go'. His body language from that moment on was so different, he laughed, he talked and he stayed to the last to meet everyone. That is what I want to end this chapter on . . . letting go.

CHAPTER 5

LEVERAGING SOCIAL NETWORKS FOR YOUR BUSINESS

IN APRIL 2008 I wrote a blog called 'Community, Intention and Tools – how to achieve leverage through software and people'.[31] So far there have been more than 4,000 views of this blog and more than eighty people have kindly added their comments to it. The message I was giving is that there are three elements to being successful inside social networks:

1. The community – the people
2. The intention – the purpose
3. The tools – the software.

So far in this book I have covered parts one and two – how to be part of a community and how to share your intention with others. Many people are afraid of using the web to build relationships and connect, this is because they see it as 'technology'. It is not, it is about the people, and by now I am sure you will have begun to understand that.

Before discussing tools, I want to share this great story I read in *Hot, Flat and Crowded* by Thomas Friedman.[32]

> A CEO had to babysit for his daughter. He was trying to read the paper but was totally frustrated by the constant interruptions. When he came across a full page of the NASA photo of earth from space, he had a brilliant idea.
>
> He ripped it into small pieces and told his daughter to try and put it together. He then settled in for what he expected to be a good half an hour of peace and quiet.
>
> But only a few minutes had gone by before the child appeared at his side with a big grin on her face.
>
> 'You've finished already?' he asked.
>
> 'Yep,' she replied.
>
> 'So how did you do it?'
>
> 'Well, there was a picture of a person on the other side, so when I put the person together, the earth got put together too.'

So, don't focus on the task, in the same way that the CEO did, focus on the people and it will all come together and make sense. You know the greatest lesson you will actually learn is that the internet mirrors real life and is just a transparent and speeded up version of the values, techniques and communication styles of the offline world.

LOOKING BACK TO LOOK FORWARDS

There have been three stages in recent internet history. I say recent, because I am focusing on the point at which it came into the mass market.

The first stage was the period of e-commerce; this is when we started Ecademy. The big buzz was 'get found on Google'. Sites were independent of one another, like individual stores in a high street. Conditions were tough because getting traffic to your site was like expecting someone to find your little store in the middle of a desert.

The second stage saw the birth of Amazon and the rise of Google. At Ecademy we had thousands of people walking around the site believing that they were the next dot-com millionaire. These were exciting times. When the dot-com bubble burst we then witnessed hundreds of people who thought they had the winning lottery ticket now searching around the floor looking for it. Dreams were smashed and the much-needed adjustment in the market happened. Reality hit hard. The lesson that was taught to everyone was that the survivors were those who saw the internet as a new business model not just a new channel to market.

The third stage, starting in 2003, saw the emergence of other social networks; we (Ecademy) were no longer alone. LinkedIn, founded in 2002 and Facebook, founded in 2004, were being talked about and confusion and hype surrounded this new world of connecting. Sharing and being found inside social networks began. With this came arguments such as 'what is spam?', wars about quantity vs quality and we saw some people, Thomas included, working hard to be at the top of LinkedIn for their country. Being connected, 'being found', was the noise being made.

In 2009, we now see the world of social media becoming mainstream news. Social media enables user-generated content. The growth in social media sites has allowed us all to become mini-publishers. Of course, sites such as Flickr, YouTube and Facebook have been around for some time but we now understand how they can help our businesses – these are not just tools for family and friends. The difficulty is understanding the rules of the game because people who are having fun don't want to have that fun interrupted by broadcasted sales messages. A subtle approach has to be adopted by the business community or they will be blocked and un-followed and the opportunity for success will be lost.

So, let's recap. E-commerce, social networking and social media are the three stages of the internet phenomenon. How have they progressed? The critical development in social media as the most recent stage is that all people and websites are integrated and linked and you can now be a publisher of your thoughts, ideas, art, pictures – basically anything. This was not possible using traditional media as for most people the possibilities were financially out of reach. The significant thought that you should absorb is the fact that sites are becoming more integrated and you must learn how to provide a journey across many terrains so that the 'researcher' or 'prospect' can find you the way they want to find you, not how you want to be found. You can increase your influence, your brand and your knowledge through these media sites, but only by playing the game in the right way. Shortly, I will discuss in detail eight magnificent social media sites, differentiated by what they do for you and who they serve. There are literally hundreds out there, in fact Thomas is on 600 social media sites, but these are the eight sites that I believe you should embrace and create your influence within.

BEING FOUND

Using search engine optimization (SEO) words, to ensure you are at the top of search, or paying Google to be there through their pay per click engine, are two of the main methods of being found online. But being simply found on Google is not enough. More conversations and activity are taking place inside social networks and social media sites than anywhere else on the internet. Search for anything on Google and the majority of the time it will take you to a community of some kind for the information. I have been on Wikipedia, LinkedIn, YouTube, Ecademy, Facebook, you name it, when researching this book. Being found is now about being found everywhere, but you need to be found with minimum time and maximum efficiency. Believe it or not, I actually don't want you to spend all your time in social media. I do know you have a life!

Thomas has learned a process of 'being found everywhere, simultaneously'. Many individuals are learning this and the brands need to emulate this fast. The term 'ubiquitous' springs to mind. When you understand the power of ubiquity, which I will teach you later, you will be able to create massive efficiencies in the way you use the social media sites to share your knowledge and thoughts.

Thankfully, you are not alone in driving traffic to your content. By being part of these communities you are one of potentially millions that are creating traffic to that site, and you gain from everyone's activity. In other words, the attractiveness of the site is increased not just by your activity and contribution, but by that of others as well. This is how you gain, this is how your content is being found when people are searching. The best analogy I can think of for this is being a concession inside a department store or being on a busy high street as opposed to having your own small shop in the middle of nowhere, where no one passes by and it is hard for people to even know you exist. Of course, you can spend money to achieve optimization on search engines and there are some excellent SEO consultants who will help you.

Don't underestimate the value of learning this subject. What social media does is provide SEO on steroids, as you are part of a bigger vibration. Social media is 'being found on the internet' not just being found on Google.

COME OUT OF YOUR COMFORT ZONE

It is very tempting to spend our lives where we feel comfortable, where life is predictable, where we know we are understood and where we can understand our surroundings. Many of us return to the same place for our holiday, many of us like to go to the same restaurant for special occasions. We become locked into 'our way of doing things'. Thomas and I are the same. Apart from when we travel, we have a coffee in the same coffee shop every Saturday morning, in the same town that we have lived in for nineteen years since we got married. I like stability, I like traditions. However, what is now happening is a shift, a change in the business world. It is a positive shift as no one can hide and our actions, values and words are transparent. It is now time to decide whether you are going to take yourself out of your comfort zone and into a new paradigm.

Later in this book is my interview with William Buist.[33] He is a 'collaborative networker for the societal web'. His use of social media is among the best and I have written up his thoughts and advice in my interview with him (see page 185). He has taught me many things and one of the most startling is 'the wider his network has grown the more efficient he has become'. This may seem counter-intuitive at first, but the greater the access to answers and to key people, the greater the acceleration in problem-solving.

Nigel Risner, a great motivational speaker who has worked

with us at many events, talks about getting out of your comfort zone.[34] In a recent talk he asked everyone in the audience to fold their arms. Some had their right hand on top of the opposite arm, others had their left. Can I ask you to do this now? Look at where yours is. He then asks you to swap this and put the other arm on top. How does that feel? Uncomfortable?

I am asking you to do the same thing throughout this book. Some things will fit comfortably with you, seem right, others will require a leap of faith and trusting me. Just do it, give it a try. What you will find is that the internet can surprise you, it will challenge your natural thoughts and encourage you to go way out of your comfort zone. It is full of people who are different to you. You cannot control their thoughts, you can only influence them.

These are some of the areas I want you to try:

1. Be open and let go of your closed past – Share your thoughts, dreams and ideas.
2. Be random and let go of being selective – Accept every contact into your life that is offered and look for new ones – don't judge.
3. Be supportive and accessible and let go of being controlling – Share your contact details, even your mobile phone number with anyone who wants it. Thomas and I have our mobile numbers on our Ecademy profile, allowing anyone to call us. The trust is there, we are saying if you want to get hold of us, we are here for you.

KNOW ME, LIKE ME, FOLLOW ME – YOUR SOCIAL FOOTPRINT

'Know me, like me, follow me', is a phrase that will become central to your online philosophy. It is all about creating your social footprint. I have created this term to help people understand a process online that they can relate to.

As you put your energy, time and passion into social media and social networks it is important for you to consider why and understand the process. While I advocate a random, open and supportive set of values, equally I feel that business people need to understand what they are doing to create the value they desire.

In the next four chapters I am going to look at the process of creating value inside the social media and social networking world. I have adopted the phrase 'know me, like me, follow me' to provide context around each area.

- You want a lot of people to *know you* exist, as part of building your personal brand. Broadcasting material when you are contributing knowledge is the social media way.
- You want to have conversations with people to build trust and get them to *like you*. Having conversations within social networks is the way to build value in your network.
- If you are doing a great job as an expert in your field of experience you would be thrilled if a number of people wanted to *follow you*, be your fan and want access to your knowledge and experience. At this level you can collaborate and find new opportunities for you and your followers.

'Know me, like me, follow me' creates the context around what you are doing to build momentum, achieve business and monitor your performance.

I have created the diagram below to graphically show a process of winning strangers over so that they become customers. Using the principles that I learnt when I read Seth Godin's book, *Permission Marketing* I have applied this to the tools, community and intention of utilizing social media. I call this Ecademy's social footprint.

Seth Godin teaches how strangers can become friends and friends can become customers. Written before social media existed, his intentions are absolutely brilliant. Few people like to sell, most like it when people come to buy. Social media can create an environment where people learn to respect and know you. Social networking enables those people to engage in conversation with you and become your followers. Those followers will contain some 'golden nuggets', some people who will become your friends, who will advocate, care and support you, on and offline, and many will become profitable relationships, customers or advocates.

What is critical to remember is that profitable relationships

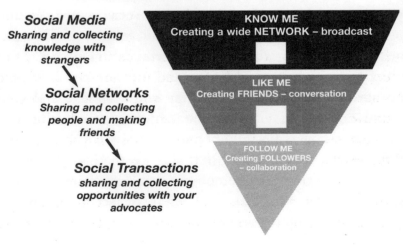

**Ecademy's Social Footprint
– From Social Media to Transactions**

Social Media
Sharing and collecting knowledge with strangers

KNOW ME
Creating a wide NETWORK – broadcast

Social Networks
Sharing and collecting people and making friends

LIKE ME
Creating FRIENDS – conversation

Social Transactions
sharing and collecting opportunities with your advocates

FOLLOW ME
Creating FOLLOWERS
– collaboration

do not have to mean a direct financial transaction. They may help you to learn, provide knowledge that you need, tell others about you, partner with you and they may buy from you. All of these results ensure your financial wealth increases. Business is not just about closing a sale with everyone you meet.

KNOW ME – COLLECTING AND SHARING KNOWLEDGE

Looking at this diagram you will see that the top of the 'funnel' is wide, it is all about utilizing the tools to 'get known'. This is traditional marketing, or brand building. It is all about creating visibility and awareness and is the twenty-first century way of broadcasting so long as you enable a connection and conversation to take place when you are sharing your knowledge.

In terms of 'new media', or as we are calling it, 'social media', this means using the tools that are available to you: writing a blog, commenting on other people's blogs, putting up videos on YouTube, adding photos to Flickr and twittering on a regular basis. Contributing on social networks and increasing your random connections and followers will add to your visibility. Using these tactical methods all help with your ability to reach a large audience and increase the influence you have across the web regarding your message and your expertise. Don't be put off by the medium you are using, just think about how you would behave and create a brand in the offline world, remembering that you are sharing knowledge not self-promoting. Also remember that everything you post remains forever, very little is deleted. In fact, it is frowned upon if you delete anything, especially if others have contributed or you are part of a conversation. The great thing is that this means that years on someone may contact you out of the blue, as everything you write is available in perpetuity. It just depends on someone searching with words that are a good match to what you have written.

Building a wide network is often about getting your message across one-to-many, and your network grows as a result of this. When you start having one-to-one 'conversations' then you are moving into the next phase of building depth.

LIKE ME – COLLECTING AND SHARING PEOPLE

Because of your raised visibility people may contact you either through commenting on a blog you wrote, sending you a private message, e-mailing, or if you are on Twitter, they will 'tweet' you. At this point it is as though they are putting their hand out to shake yours and say 'Hi'. People do this in many ways; some do it well, whereas others are clumsy and come across as 'spamming'. We have to remember this is a new world that everyone is learning and be tolerant of the styles that some people use.

It is always good to reply to messages, although you can filter at this point and reply to ones that look like they are interested in conversation. This is where you will begin to create depth in your network. This is your opportunity to build trust and a relationship based on knowing one another and hopefully liking each other. It is important to have depth in your network – a wide network only reflects your visibility, whereas the depth of your network reflects your credibility.

Depth of networks can be measured by how many people have left you a testimonial, the number of comments you have and interestingly, also by how many people have taken the step to 'follow you' on Twitter or join a group or club you have created in a social network such as Facebook, Ecademy or LinkedIn.

FOLLOW ME – ENABLING A SOCIAL TRANSACTION

As you come down the 'funnel' you are creating relevance. Relevance is harder to achieve. Those that do contact you and begin to form a deeper understanding of you have indicated that there is something about you that interests or intrigues them. Getting to the next level and having a 'following' is the toughest part, but it is where the greatest opportunity lies. It is through having a 'following' that you will be able to find opportunities, collaborate and have meaningful discussions with people similar to you.

Later, in Chapter ten, I discuss the benefit of leading clubs or groups. This is like creating your own mini-social network. It takes leadership, passion and tenacity to run a club, but the rewards are high if done well.

UNDERSTANDING YOURSELF

Before you really throw yourself into social media I suggest you consider the following three questions:

1. What type of networker are you?
2. What is your natural communication style?
3. What is your expertise?

WHAT TYPE OF NETWORKER ARE YOU?

In 2005, a brilliant man who we met on Ecademy called Bjørn Guldager from Denmark, explained to Thomas and me that he had a theory, based on years of teaching networking, about people being different types of networkers. I have taken this excerpt from Bjørn's blog.[35/36] Think about which one you are and consider whether it is working for you.

The Passive Networker does not want to network at all. They may have a feeling that they are missing out by not networking, but really, their 'world of one' is quite big enough for them.

The Conservative Networker will network, but only with people with whom they have a long 'common story' (e.g. members of the same club) or when sufficient trust has been built up over a long period of time.

The Reactive Networker will be open to new proposals and indeed networking relationships, but will be selective and thus keep control over their network – and they don't expand it much on their own account.

The Proactive Networker actually 'crosses the comfort zone border' and goes out to develop the network in the way they want, but is selective about the project they dive into and the people they approach. Focus is on quality or priority and they take responsibility for making it happen.

The Hyperactive Networker networks with anyone

over anything and believes strongly in quantity and possibly even 'random connections' as they may lead to something at some point. Quantity and energy are two characteristics but there is less focus on priority.

You will have an affinity with one of these types and that will be your comfort zone, but as you know, I am advocating that you step out of this comfort zone and push yourself to a level where you may increase serendipity and allow the random to happen in your life.

HOW TO PROGRESS AND EMBRACE THE CHALLENGE

I asked Bjørn how he felt people could progress through to the next level of networking at times when it would be beneficial to them. We cannot expect people to change their personality or personal values so far as networking is concerned, but perhaps we can encourage change when it would help them achieve a goal. Bjørn explained that the challenge, whether in a private, professional or networking context, varies depending on which type(s) you are – often people find themselves using aspects from two or even three of the networking types, as many are fortunately able to act according to the situation they are in.

These are the challenges that Bjørn has witnessed from each type. Each type has to adapt to certain situations:

- For the **passive** networker, the challenge lies in realizing that networking might actually be of benefit at times. For example, when asking advice regarding a job or lending a friend some money, trusting that they will return it. They may not like the term 'networking' but they are doing it at times all the same.

- For the **conservative** networker, the challenge could be starting up new relations based on 'perceived good intentions' from the other person, rather than having to go through years of knowing each other before the comfort level is high enough.

- For the **reactive** networker, who is used to prioritizing and being 'in control', the challenge is taking the initiative, rather than waiting for others to step forwards and make contact. Accepting that a wider network may have value will make a difference to the reactive networker.

- For the **proactive** networker, the challenge is to look at the wider opportunities around them and be less selective in their networking. This attitude can blinker them to knowledge and people that may help them advance and adapt to the new business opportunities that exist.

- For the **hyperactive** networker, the challenge is to start relaxing and enjoying exchanges with the existing relations, not always focusing on building a network, but also spending time with people and getting to know them well.

WHAT IS YOUR NATURAL COMMUNICATION STYLE?

In July 2008 I was at an event and met a really good man, James Knight. James is an American living in the UK. He had just joined Ecademy and the two of us got on like a house on fire immediately.

Within a short time, James had taught me some very valuable lessons in communication. Based on his knowledge of Carl Jung,[37] James had developed a short questionnaire comprising ten questions that focused on communication style, called IMA™ Personal Profiling.[38] Glenn Watkins, our CEO, liked this so much that he embedded the code in our site and now members can link to the questions and display the results directly on their profile. It is astonishing what they reveal.

I want to list now the four communication styles that people have. They are called 'High' because they are the dominant style, of course we all have a bit of everything that we use to adapt to different situations.

IMA HIGH BLUE

A person with this style bases their communication on depth. They like to form relationships and they are non-assertive. They like conversation and tend to keep control of their network and don't go for a wide network unless they have time to nurture it.

If you want to communicate with someone who has this style:

- Be pleasant
- Be non-assertive
- Be consistent
- Be selfless
- Be open
- Be supportive of their feelings
- Be sincere.

IMA HIGH YELLOW

These are the hypernetworkers. They are comfortable with wide networks, they are communicators rather than conversationalists, they are often the early adopters of the new social media sites and they cannot get enough of all the tools that allow them to build their network and get their message across. They are in danger of being accused of spam, but they are being vindicated for this behaviour now.

The High Yellow is an assertive character, likes to get things done quickly and they will find the most efficient pathway through to gaining visibility.

If you want to communicate with someine who has this style:

- Be flexible
- Be quick-paced
- Be positive
- Be open
- Be generous with your praise
- Be supportive of their ideas
- Have fun!

IMA HIGH RED

These people want a return on investment. They look for practical solutions and feel time starved. The High Reds are great at delegating and collaborating. They have no time for people, the task is what they focus on; rather than being relationship focused they want to get things done. They don't want lengthy conversations and they want you to respect their time.

If you want to communicate with this style:

- Be practical
- Be brief
- Be assertive
- Be to the point
- Be supportive of their goals
- Be respectful of their time
- Show strength.

IMA HIGH GREEN

High Greens are analytical, they want to understand what can be achieved, they take a logical approach to their networking and are focused, like the High Reds, on the task more than the people. They are non-assertive and, like the High Blues, need you to be supportive of their thoughts (the High Blue wants you to support their feelings). High Greens love information.

If you want to communicate with someone who has this style:

- Be time-disciplined
- Be logical
- Be prepared
- Be respectful of rules
- Be supportive of their thoughts
- Be structured and well organized
- Be precise.

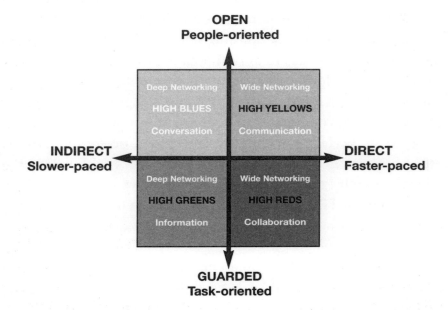

HOW THIS WORKS FOR US AS A TEAM ON ECADEMY

It is interesting for us as a team running Ecademy as Thomas is a High Yellow; he is our hypernetworker. I am a High Blue, comfortable in smaller groups where I can have deep conversations. Glenn, our CEO, is a High Red, i.e. highly commercial. Julian Bond, our CTO, is a High Green, focused on diligently looking after the website, creating new codes and managing the detail.

I can drive Glenn mad with my need for chat and conversation, he can drive me mad with his abrupt, task-focused behaviour. Thomas drives us all mad with his incessant need to build networks and Julian, well, I guess he is the only sane one! The most important aspect of this knowledge of communication styles is that you can learn and adapt to those around you. You cannot change the way people communicate, but you can change the way you empathize and adapt to their style.

Knowing that someone is a High Red helps you to understand that the relationship side of networking will be secondary in their desire to fulfil a task. You will know that a High Blue would like you to read their profile and comment on something that is important to them. Accepting that a High Yellow may, in your interpretation, 'spam' you will enable you to trust in the fact that they are still a good person to know, they are just in a hurry and want to network with a lot of people. Finally, give time to a High Green, who could be the detail you need in your business and add a lot of value to what you do and who you know. I recommend that you profile everyone on your organization and even learn to spot the styles of people you hope to do business with.

Adapting your style to the different types of people around you will help you achieve a great deal more. Of course, it is hard to see what type of IMA everyone is, as not everyone has done this questionnaire. However, do it yourself by visiting Ecademy or www.potentialunlimited.com and then learn how to spot these people just from understanding their communication style.

WHAT IS YOUR EXPERTISE?

I covered this earlier, but this is critical. Until you understand what your expertise is and how you want to influence and build a network around you, you will not be able to create relevance or a following. Without having something that people can relate to you, it will be harder to create advocates, build a collaborative team around you, spot opportunities and make your time online productive.

A major theme throughout this book is the need to share knowledge. Knowledge is your greatest asset inside social media and you will accumulate knowledge the more you network with people. Experience combined with knowledge gives you credibility, while sharing your knowledge will give you visibility.

Spend time understanding what expertise you have and then begin the journey online of building that knowledge base and demonstrating your expertise. I will be talking about this a great deal later in the book as this is an essential part of your toolkit to build attraction inside social media.

UNDERSTAND YOURSELF AND THEN TAKE TIME TO UNDERSTAND OTHERS

Write down what your expertise is and what type of knowledge you want to gain to make your expertise even stronger. This will lead you to consider the wider aspects of your expertise and perhaps the intention you have for helping others.

Consider what type of networker you are and consider stepping out of your comfort zone to do something that will raise your visibility and display your credibility.

Finally, take the IMA questionnaire to discover your communication style and look at the people you know and understand them. 'Birds of a feather flock together', so they say. You will get along best with people like you, but are those people potential customers for your products? Also, your business is not just about sales, it is about learning and developing your ideas. Ecademy is successful because we have all four types of communicator on our board. We came together because we could see how the other people could complement our weaknesses. Don't just network with people like you.

Understanding these three aspects of yourself – your networking type, your communication style and your expertise – will help you to understand how to utilize social media and it may highlight some of the ways in which you need to move out of your comfort zone to fully maximize its potential.

CHAPTER 6

KNOW ME, LIKE ME, FOLLOW ME

THE NOISE OF the internet is all around us and trying to decide what to focus on may be one of the reasons so many procrastinate rather than dive in. You need to know which communities serve which people, which tools are effective for business use and which social media and social networking sites to trust in terms of their ability to serve you into the future.

There have been thousands of casualties along the way, sites that have sprung up, made a lot of noise and then disappeared. Funding and running a site that serves millions of people around the world cannot be underestimated.

The competition for an audience to gain attention has been immense and this has given rise to the free economy, an expectation that much of the information and tools on the internet should be supplied for free. This expectation affects you too – the free economy is everywhere. The gain for you is that you don't have to pay for many of the tools; the downside is that this means you have to filter out a lot of noise.

Another consideration is the way in which sites have

decided to focus their attention, either on the tools, which I call utilities, or on the people, which I call community. In this chapter I will provide you with some examples of sites that I like and use and that I know are the market leaders in most cases. However, there are several hundred sites out there. Your job is to decide which sites you intuitively like and where you will find people you are happy to be associated with.

FREE ECONOMY

Throughout this book I have talked about contribution, intention and helping others. There is more to it than just being kind. It is said that 'there is no such thing as a free lunch'. It is also said that 'no kind gesture is a selfless one'. I will explain how this applies to the free economy.

One of the toughest aspects of building Ecademy privately has been accepting that more than 95 per cent of our users do not want to pay for the access to people and knowledge we provide. I guess if we had taken investment from venture capitalists this would be less painful. For us, we have needed to very clearly understand the reasons why people won't pay and we have also had to learn to value every member, whether they pay or not. I talked about this in terms of contribution currency earlier. Everyone has something to contribute to a community and a business, some in terms of finance, others with their advocacy and their content.

Interestingly for us, the members that don't pay us a penny invite more members into Ecademy than those that do. They not only contribute with their thoughts and knowledge by adding content, they also help us with our marketing.

In 2004, Chris Anderson wrote an article in *Wired* magazine where he talked about the 'long tail'.[39/40] He described a strategy for businesses that distributed their goods at high volume to a large number of people but at a low price (or free) in order to gain a great deal more at the 'end of the tail'. This phrase and concept has become commonplace in the social media industry. It helps many understand how to achieve sales from a smaller group of people from providing free or low-cost value at the beginning of the journey, which involves a large group. Now termed the 'freemium' business model, this is the concept of combining free products or services with premium ones. The freemium business model was first articulated by venture capitalist Fred Wilson in March 2006.[41]

It is worth noting that Chris Anderson is an economist and editor of *Wired*,[42] and so is embedded in the new media world and is an advocator of the 'free economy'. On 26 February 2009, he announced he would be running a free summit. The marketing material on this summit stated that 'we are looking for individuals or organizations interested in presenting case studies on how they've used "free" as a part of their business model'. This theory is becoming mainstream and has been the pillar of the social media and social networking sites. It is now becoming an important message to individuals who want to build their brand and business.

While researching this subject I came across this quote from Thomas Jefferson, US president at the turn of the nineteenth century.[43]

> If nature has made any one thing less susceptible than all others of exclusive property, it is the action of the thinking power called an idea, which an individual may exclusively possess as long as he keeps it to himself; but the moment it is divulged, it forces itself into the possession of every one, and the receiver cannot

dispossess himself of it. Its peculiar character, too, is that no one possesses the less, because every other possesses the whole of it. He who receives an idea from me, receives instruction himself without lessening mine; as he who lights his taper at mine, receives light without darkening me.

Basically, Jefferson was saying that once an idea has been born and told it can no longer remain the property of that person. They just have to live with the knowledge that they were the creator and recognize that it costs nothing to give away an idea. Of course he is not considering the cost of the research and development and more recent economics and laws around intellectual property, but perhaps the modern philosophies of collaboration, sharing and the need to provide free value is bringing about what Jefferson could see over 200 years ago.

THE RISE OF CONVERSATION MARKETING

Broadcast marketing relied on many people seeing what *you* wanted them to see. Conversation marketing is the evolution of this form of marketing. The ability for people to interact inside communities and to share ideas and opinions has created a trusted source of communication. This rise has happened alongside the loss of respect for many major companies and individuals within them. Increasingly people are relying on conversations to form trust.

In my interview with Graham Jones, internet psychologist and one of the UK's most successful bloggers, I enjoyed hearing him say that the world is returning to old values of asking a friend to give them the answer. Graham explained that when the web was formed for the mass market, Google became the place to gather information. However, when forums and subsequently communities became significant, the power of community began to overtake the power of search.

Graham shared with me that, 'Pre-internet, you would ask a friend or colleague if they knew someone who could help you. They may have known someone. If not, you probably would have resorted to the *Yellow Page*s. When Google came along, many of us abandoned asking our friends and colleagues for help; instead we independently went to Google and searched for a supplier. Over time we started to realize that this did not necessarily mean you found the best person or the most reliable and trusted. The ability for anyone to buy their way to the top of Google or to utilize search engine optimization just meant that those at the top were clever at using search engines. We realized once again that it is recommendations from people that secure us a good supplier, and once again community became a critical resource, just like it always was.'

Conversation marketing is becoming the most critical aspect of a company's marketing strategy. Getting people to talk about you will provide the brand exposure that you need to create a reputation and a level of trust. We know that broadcast is dying, as less and less is being spent on television advertising and even advertising in communities. The largest brands such as Coca-Cola and British Airways are spending more and more of their budget on understanding how to engage and talk to their 'audience' inside communities, seeing their customers as an audience rather than as end-users. British Airways have now created a community for people travelling between New York and London called Metrotwin, which is a community for people to share their experiences. Looking at the front page of www.metrotwin.com you see, 'Our recommendations come from a network of experts and locals: bloggers, online communities based in New York and London.' Encouraging conversation around people's travel experiences is their priority, there is little broadcasting of flight costs and times but conversations inevitably create transactions.

CREATING YOUR PRESENCE INSIDE COMMUNITIES

What we have seen since the 'user' has had the ability to generate content is a massive increase online in the provision of free advice, free events and the sharing of knowledge. It is your opportunity to leverage the 'free economy' and create your own 'long tail'.

User-generated content (UGC) symbolizes the core of social media. UGC is what we all have to do now – from writing blogs, twittering, recording podcasts, to producing videos and publishing our knowledge in downloadable pdfs. As an expert you need to be creating and distributing as much of this knowledge and content for free as possible. Your challenge is to find the product or service that you can 'sell' at the end of this 'long tail'.

UNDERSTANDING KNOW ME, LIKE ME, FOLLOW ME

In the following three chapters I am going to look in detail at the 'know me, like me, follow me' concept. I interviewed more than forty people, either over the phone, through Skype, e-mail or face to face. These interviews provide in-depth insights to give you some real case studies as to how experienced people are utilizing social media. Receiving their knowledge has been a tremendous learning experience for me. It is quite amazing what is being achieved through social media and each one of them is committed to the contribution of their knowledge and their desire for an open, transparent, random and unstructured world. It is through these beliefs that magic seems to happen to them all.

I was determined to divide the social media sites into the three categories –'know me', 'like me' and 'follow me' – due to my own desire for a neat structured world, but I was naïve in my depth of understanding. Of course, I get reminded every day that the amazing thing about this new world is everyone can tailor their world around what suits them. A site may be used for broadcast by one person, but for conversation by another.

USING OR BELONGING

A key aspect of how you will feel about a site is whether you feel at home there. There will be one dominant place for you where you like the people, where you trust the content, where the content is perfect for you, where you fit in and where the tools of the site sit most intuitively for you. Of course the offline world is no different. We cannot all like the same hotel, wine bar, club or sporting activity.

For me, this was obvious when I worked in the corporate world in the early 1990s. I lived in a town in the south of England called Farnham (in fact I still do) and I worked in a town called High Wycombe, about a 50-mile journey each day. I cared deeply about Farnham, its people, the environment, whether there was a litter or graffiti problem, whether there were problems with late-night drinking and noise on the streets. It is my community, I want to feel safe and I want to contribute. High Wycombe on the other hand, was the 'utility' that served me; providing me with a road system, a desk and a place to get my sandwich at lunchtime. That was it. There was no emotion towards High Wycombe, I wasn't worried if there was a drug problem or graffiti. Trust and companionship was not my priority. I came and went; in a sense I purely 'took' from this town. High Wycombe was someone else's community.

You will treat many sites in the same way. No matter how much you want to provide a cohesive set of values and contribute across all platforms, it is very hard to create community across them all. This would require you to have conversations and friendships in each place, something that could be achieved, and I applaud you if you can, but time may be the barrier for this. My research has shown me that some people see sites as a marketing place for visibility and place their emphasis on an alternative site for their deeper friendships. These sites appear to be less about marketing and more about knowledge and support. Thomas says, 'Community is not a thing, it is an atmosphere, it is an emotion and it is a feeling.' Community is very special, but it cannot be forced on you, you either become part of it or you don't, based on how you 'feel' about the atmosphere and the trust you have for it.

MILE WIDE AND MILE DEEP NETWORKING

In September of 2008 I wrote a blog called 'Mile Wide or Mile Deep Networking'.[44] With over 110 comments and over 4,400 views from within Ecademy alone, it is one of my most popular blogs. In this blog I explored the two aspects of networking online that create the most debate and arguments – that of having a wide, large network or a deep, smaller network. The blog was also accompanied by a poll, a link inside the blog that gave readers and commentators an opportunity to say what type of networking they preferred – wide, deep or wide and deep.[45] The results from the 368 people who voted were that only 9 per cent were focused on having a wide network, the other 91 per cent wanted to have a deep network, of which 54 per cent said that both wide and deep were important to them.

Do you build mile wide networks? (I like all random and global contacts and all messages are welcomed.)   9%

Do you build mile deep networks? (I filter on relevance and ignore some messages from strangers.)   91%

Of those who answered 'Yes' to the second question, do you build wide and deep networks? (I welcome all contacts, pro-actively connect and also take time to get to know my network.)   54%

LEAVING YOUR UNIQUE FOOTPRINT

My research for this book has given me the most tremendous insight into how people use social media and what has become abundantly clear is that everyone uses it in a different way. Like a thumbprint, your footprints around the sites are unique to you. The way you choose to browse, navigate, observe or get involved will be like no other and the level at which you choose to engage on a site will be individual to you. One person will use a site for deep, meaningful conversations, while another will purely see the same site as a utility, a place to create visibility. The best advice is not to judge the motives of anyone, but get close to those you respect and like wherever they are. Always maintain your standards and values as you will bump into people in many places and if you create distrust in one place this reputation will carry over to all the other sites too. If people like you, this will become viral across the internet.

EXAMINING A HYPERNETWORKER

I am going to focus now on a case study of Thomas Power, in particular his role as a hypernetworker. Thomas is on hundreds of social media sites, using some for friendship, some for knowledge, some for seeking out new contacts, some for speaking to a close group of experts, some for marketing and some for fun. Thomas is truly a social media junkie. With such a strong passion for what the internet can do for others, he speaks and shares all the time. Despite having a large network, Thomas is achieving depth, trust and friendship. As a family we can travel the world and stay with people in hundreds of cities thanks to the way that Thomas has contributed, online and offline, to people's lives.

I am not being sycophantic here, I am writing this because I want to illustrate that having a wide network does not by any means reduce your ability to build trust or know people well. In fact, the opposite is true. Because of Thomas's wide network he is able to connect people to information and people so fast he is constantly providing value to others.

THE MIDDLEMAN

Thomas says 'the internet is the vehicle to follow the best minds'. He sees the internet as a place where he can access the minds of people and understand what they are thinking so he can know what to do next. Thomas is not a maker of news, nor is he a global thought leader. What he wants to achieve is to find the best people in social media across the world, connect with them, subscribe to their blogs and 'feeds' and help anyone in his network access their information. Acting as a filter, Thomas is the 'middleman' between knowledge and people, connecting people to the knowledge they need to adapt, innovate and survive. Thomas is a 'fast follower', bridging the gap between the innovators and creators and the mass market. This is Ecademy's role as a result.

Once Thomas has found information, he then shares it across multiple social media platforms to 'feed' his network. Random connection, random knowledge, but the thread of relevance is helping people to keep on top of what is going on in the world.

Thomas's background is in marketing. He studied the subject at college and became marketing manager at Amstrad, the largest PC manufacturer in the 1980s, owned by Sir Alan Sugar. Thomas then went on to create his own marketing company aged twenty-three, at that time providing telemarketing services for IT companies. The internet came into his life in 1994, aged thirty, thanks to the founder of AKQA, Ajaz Ahmed, who came to our house as a young man for dinner. Ever since then he has been hooked and mesmerized by this new media world and how businesses can build their brands and get known and trusted.

It is no surprise when you read this journey of Thomas's that the internet is such a fascination to him. Combine this with his love of networking and his desire to connect people and you can see why Thomas spends over eighty hours a week social networking, either face to face or online.

The most startling thing that Thomas said to me when I interviewed him for this section of the book was that his focus is on meeting people. The offline world is still the world that Thomas likes best. He wants to meet those he follows and those that follow him face to face whenever he can. Thomas has travelled to over fifty countries meeting Ecademy members and his love is to have one-to-one meetings, train or speak wherever he lands. What Thomas wants is typical of most. Nothing can replace physically meeting a person – it is a sign of respect, it is a commitment and it is the best way to really build trust and friendship.

Social media enables Thomas to meet and follow thousands of people online, but his favourite tool on Ecademy is the 'events' tools, where people can book meetings and events and he can go along. Ecademy has over 500 meetings displayed in its events diary each month, across hundreds of cities. Thanks to the online world, we can find out a great deal about people before we meet, in many instances people who come together as a result of forming an online friendship. Blogs, videos, photos and messages reduce the amount of small talk and allow people to very quickly bond or become commercial partners. Your reputation is already fairly solid, visibility and credibility have already been achieved, in effect you are already 'known'. Meeting and talking enables a deeper level of engagement, which can accelerate people into 'being liked' and trusted.

FOLLOWING THE BEST MINDS

While Ecademy is without doubt Thomas's online home, his depth and his place to 'belong', FriendFeed is the site that Thomas uses to follow the best minds. The following is taken from their home page: 'FriendFeed helps you discover and discuss interesting stuff that your friends and family find on the web.' Once you have found the experts you want to follow, it automatically picks up their content from over fifty sites, including Facebook, Flickr and Twitter, and feeds it to you to save you time and brings you information in real time. FriendFeed is a content aggregator by person, a brilliant concept that is taking off well among the early adopters.

After more than eighteen months, spending hours reading content on FriendFeed, Thomas has now identified the 120 people he most admires in social media. FriendFeed has allowed him to aggregate these people into one place, with all their content on all social media sites being fed into this one site (the term used for this activity is 'streaming'). Reducing the time Thomas needs to spend surfing around and entering multiple platforms, he can now visit one site, FriendFeed, and read everything that these 120 people are saying and thinking.

FriendFeed is not just a place to extract information. Thomas has also set a feed up into FriendFeed that 'streams' his thoughts and links into FriendFeed. In the same way that

Thomas is following people, Thomas has over 1,200 people 'following' him. At any time, Thomas can look at a list of people that 'he finds most interesting' based on his clicks to their content, and equally, he can see a list of people that find him most interesting, thereby knowing what type of people are enjoying his feeds. This data is further enhanced by the fact that he can also see which sites those he follows and those that follow him are spending their time on, enabling him to see what the up-and-coming sites are. Critically this also tells him what 'the best minds are using'.

It is no surprise as I write this book that Twitter dominates the social media world as the newest and most leading-edge site in 2009. Twitter allows random connections, encouraging openness and transparency, a philosophy held by Ecademy, Thomas and me. This reflects that people are moving their value systems towards these ways of communicating. This is a major leap forward in business. While Google takes you to the knowledge, Twitter randomly takes you to the people with the knowledge.

MONETIZING YOUR ONLINE ACTIVITY

The fundamental aspect of the hours that Thomas spends in social media is how he can ensure that through this hobby, passion, addiction and, dare I say, obsession, he can actually make money. This is a problem for literally hundreds of people at the leading edge of social media. For Thomas, he has Ecademy as his business, run by Glenn Watkins, Ecademy's CEO. Thomas can stay outside of the walls of Ecademy and add value to it by being random, unstructured, connected and giving. All with the comfort of knowing that 'at the end of the long tail' Ecademy will achieve more traffic and increased credibility and trust because of his interaction and engagement. Apart from traffic coming to Ecademy via search engines, the big three – Facebook, LinkedIn and Twitter – are the biggest contributors to Ecademy's traffic. Being seen inside these networks is feeding Ecademy with more users and members. Thomas contributes to Ecademy as a by-product of his activity elsewhere, but of course, that is not what he is doing this for. He is involved in social media because it is what he loves, his intentions are not focused on the money, but on the sharing of information. In Thomas's words, 'Money is the output, connecting people is the input.'

UTILIZING THE SITES

Thomas has a very clear mind with regard to what he can achieve inside his favourite social media sites. He has a plan and he executes these processes and tasks diligently. Looking at it simplistically, this is the order of priority for Thomas's day and time:

Ecademy   **For depth, relationships and meeting people**
• Meet new people at events and private meetings – offline.
• Blog to ask questions of the community – as and when needed.
• Comment on blogs to supply answers and connections.
• Discuss, opinionate and share inside groups of interest such as the Twitter Club and the BlackStar Private Club of members.
• Blog once a month with knowledge to his

entire network – Ecademy allows subscribers to send out an announcement once a month to your whole network.

• 'Tweet' blogs and people he reads about on Ecademy.

• Aggregate all his feeds into one community for optimization and his 'home' on the web.

FriendFeed   **Aggregating experts and gossiping**

• Reading, learning, analyzing and sharing 'likes' and gossip about social media news.

Socialmedian   **Accessing knowledge**

• Sharing news clips with his network.

Twitter   **Alerting his network to all the latest stories and people**

• Group-shared SMS on the internet.

• Advocating the best people and information in real time from anywhere.

Facebook   **For research**

• Watching the way Facebook users are engaging, sharing and what they are talking about.

• Reading the 'news feed', a live stream of what his friends are doing and saying.

LinkedIn   **For building network width and branding**

• Building a global network, connecting and passing business connections.

• Number one for number of testimonials in the world.

YouTube	**Learning through video**
	• Watching videos of experts in business and social media for knowledge.
Flickr	**Sharing experiences**
	• Sharing pictures from his face to face meetings from around the world, feeding them into Ecademy to thank people for their time and share his travels and events with others. These photos are the tool Thomas loves the most – they capture the moment, they capture 'people history'. It is no surprise that sharing and tagging photos is also huge on Facebook.

These eight sites provide Thomas with knowledge and people. These are the two most important aspects of the internet:

1. Connecting you to information
2. Connecting you to the people that hold that knowledge.

SHARING AND ADVOCATING

I described Thomas as the 'middleman'. In his interview this came across very clearly as his driver – advocating and sharing information. The powerful output of this is that by being part of Thomas's large network people become 'known'. The best social media experts know this and their intention is always focused on sharing and promoting others. This is why self-promotion and selling does not work in this world. Understanding the difference between self-promotion and self-publication is the most subtle lesson of online life. It takes time, commitment and empathy to learn this, but if your core values and your understanding sit comfortably with this philosophy this will be more natural than it appears.

Self-promotion: 'Hey look at me, I know everything and I am brilliant.'

Self-publishing: 'Can I help you to learn from me? If I can help, here I am.'

or

'Follow these great people, they are really smart.'

Which person do you want to be?

In Chapter eight I will look at the power of advocacy in more detail. Surrounding yourself with people who advocate you because they like, trust and know you, can help others. People do not advocate those who self-promote.

KNOWLEDGE – YOUR STARTING POINT AND YOUR POWER

Throughout all my research for this book, one thing has dominated every aspect; that is the power of knowledge. Knowledge is defined in the *Oxford English Dictionary* as 'Expertise, and skills acquired by a person through experience or education'. Knowledge is the key to you or your organization creating a brand inside social media, but it is incredibly hard to define what your knowledge is.

On a training course recently, I asked everyone to introduce themselves. This was achieved by everyone with great flair and clarity. Everyone seemed to know how to get themselves across with passion and create a good feeling around them. No one broadcasted themselves, no one treated it as their 'sixty-second elevator pitch'. We all understood who was in the room and what each person did with their lives.

Ninety minutes into my training, having covered the philosophies and marketing aspects of social media, I asked everyone to pick up their pen and write down what knowledge they have that they could share with others. I asked them to make this relevant to how they earn their living. I watched as a set of successful, forty-plus-year-old people became stressed and frustrated, staring at a blank piece of paper. Only one man out of ten attendees wrote anything down.

If I had asked 'how do you make a living?', 'what do you sell?' or 'create an advert on your products and services' it would have been easy. But asking people to consider what knowledge they have is tough. Why is that? Once you know what knowledge you have your social media contribution becomes clearer and has greater purpose.

Let's look at what I have covered in this chapter:

- The free economy – how to create income at the end of the 'long tail'
- User-generated content – creating your content on the web
- Social networks and websites – knowing how to use them – as a utility or community
- The size of your network and why it matters
- The role of a middleman, between people and the knowledge.

All of these aspects lead to one point of leverage – knowledge. The knowledge you want to be known for, what people and knowledge you have access to, who you know and what they know. You cannot begin to make sense of social media until you understand what you are an expert in. Once you have decided that, you can build a network around you that will feed you with the latest news and thoughts, help you build your reputation and advocate you to anyone they know that should read your content, connect with you and meet you.

So consider what you are selling and what knowledge you have that makes you so good at providing your product or service. Think about why people are attracted to you, what you share with them and what you contribute to them. Now think about how you can build that knowledge every day and be known for being the oracle in your industry and in your chosen community.

In Thomas's case he has focused on social media, building knowledge that can be shared with a network of business people on Ecademy. Ecademy is his community, his home on the net, the other sites act as a set of resources for him, providing him with knowledge and people.

In the next chapter I am going to share some case studies of people who are sharing their expertise through blogging and YouTube, two key channels for knowledge distribution.

CHAPTER 7

KNOW ME – CREATING YOUR SOCIAL MEDIA FOOTPRINT

We WILL NOW begin the process of building your network with a strategy that will help you create profitable relationships. The first part of this is 'know me'. 'Know me' is the aspect of social media that is closest to the traditional world that you may be used to. This stage is about your marketing, it is about building your brand and creating a reputation.

Being known is critical. It is through having a trusted brand that is wide and distributed across many platforms, that you will be found by people wanting access to your mind, knowledge and connections.

'Know me' is about 'one-to-many', finding a way to publish your expertise in a way that creates followers and trust. One person, YOU, reaching out to MANY. Once your blog is read and 'followed' by many, in a wide geographical area, you are achieving a brand, a reputation that allows you to be known. Surely that is what we all want? This builds your reputation, which creates attraction and helps to raise your profile. You cannot focus on depth. Your aim is to contribute by sharing knowledge. Those that want to engage with you will do so, and then you may decide to move to 'like me' and become a friend to them.

WHY PEOPLE WORRY ABOUT BUILDING A LARGE NETWORK

There are a number of misconceptions about creating a wide network and I want to cover them here to help you overcome any fears you may have. I have featured the two most common concerns; that width means you do not contribute to others and that you do not have time to manage a large network.

1. If you have a wide network you cannot be a giver – really?
A damaging assumption many people have is that those with a large network are 'using' the networks, that they are collecting names, that they are taking and not giving. Don't be one of those people who make this judgement.

Thomas has a much larger network than I do. He also loves to connect and build networks across multiple social media platforms. At the time of writing I have 5,300 in my Ecademy network, Thomas has 45,526. If we look at the depth of my network, 7 per cent of my network have written a testimonial, whereas only 1.3 per cent of Thomas's have. But looking at this in real terms it means that I have received 372 testimonials from people who have taken the time to thank me for my help, but Thomas has received 573. Thomas has the appreciation of 200 more people than I have. Perhaps this means that having a wide network enables Thomas to connect and share with more people and therefore contribute to more. Take this across all the networks that Thomas is on, and considering that he is currently the number one person in the world for testimonials on LinkedIn, with 700, Thomas does not lack contribution when it comes to helping his networks.

2. Managing a large network takes too much time

You will read later in my interview with William Buist, that a wide network has made him more efficient (see page 185). William is someone I admire as a great collaborator and advocator. He said to me that as his network has become larger, he has more time on his hands. This is the reverse of what you would think. One of the main barriers for people creating a wide network is that they think this will take too much time to manage. William confirmed to me that through his business model and his processes the more people he has access to, the more his business has grown and the more efficient he is. Having access to minds, knowledge and people speeds up solving problems, finding information and increases the opportunities. Graham Jones, one of the UK's top bloggers and an internet psychologist, confirmed that he never sells, he only delivers. His customers come to him because of his blog and his wide network. He has already achieved a level of credibility and visibility that cuts down the prospecting and closing time of the sales process.

CAN YOU PROCRASTINATE ANY LONGER?

Whenever I get the feeling that someone is not getting on board with social media and networking I have great empathy for how they are feeling but deep concern that they are not going to be able to survive in the business world beyond the next five years. The generation that is embracing social media and networks is ensuring they will be part of a whole new way of being found, doing business and making business friends. To demonstrate this I want to share with you four comments from my daughter Hannah, aged sixteen.

> 'I have Facebook set up to send all my notifications, friends' requests, etc. to my BlackBerry so I can check them all the time.'

What does this tell you about her behaviour? Hannah is living in a world where she is connected to her friends in real time, all the time. Information is coming to her in small nuggets throughout her day that tell her what is happening in her friends' lives. 'Nat has passed her driving test', 'Matt has lost his wallet', 'NJ is on the bus to college for an exam'. This information does not phase her, but when she can, she will text them or contact them on Facebook and congratulate them or ask them how they did in their exam. This enables Hannah to be caring, interested and in touch.

The significant aspect of this for you to absorb is that this is easy. The technology is there to help her be a better friend and give a helping hand. We all have to achieve this level of communication now to embrace our 'friends' and know when they need us. (Remember, friends in your context are your business friends.)

> 'Sometimes at college, if we're discussing someone I don't know, we search them on Facebook on my phone.'

Hannah is always embracing and looking for new people to know. She expands her network, looks for ways to add value to her friendships and creates new friendships while nurturing her old ones.

We need to understand that random, trusted contacts are good – embracing and sharing people is the way this generation see life. They do not judge, they do not filter; they can work in a world of random, open and supportive values. This is their philosophy and the technology enables it.

'People use Facebook to sell stuff and advertise events all the time. I sold my old iPod in January over Facebook by just putting it in my Facebook status.'

Hannah was able to sell her iPod within twenty minutes of getting a new one for Christmas. She sold it to a friend of a friend because she was in a trusted environment where people knew Hannah's values and knew they were safe to recommend her. It cost her nothing to sell it and 'Luke', the buyer, was delighted.

We will increasingly do business in this way. Social networks enable business to happen in a random way that occurs because of the reputation you have, not because of what you are or what you do. Relying on job titles, control and targeted selling will be an old method of marketing and selling for this generation. In the future, commerce will sit on top of community, the two will be entwined.

'I have a group of eight friends from my old school. We have a thread on Facebook that we have had for a year now, which we use to update each other and give each other help with different things. It's basically a really long e-mail but it's a really good way of keeping connected.'

Hannah is part of a small group of people that stay close and intimate long after the 'event' that they shared brought them together. These eight girls were at school together, now they have gone their separate ways to college, but they are able to stay in touch and keep sharing and caring for one another. When Hannah leaves college she might have 900 contacts, when she leaves university she may have 1,200. This is 1,200 people who will join 1,200 companies. Consider that network and consider how much lower the cost of doing business will be for the next generation.

BECOMING A BLOGGER

One method you can use to become known and respected is blogging. I have discovered that blogging can be a hobby, a business, a marketing strategy and a way of having conversation inside communities. There are no fixed rules around how you approach blogging, as long as you remember that it is 'not about self-promotion, it is self-publication'.

Louis Gray on the west coast of America is a wonderful example of how blogging can add another dimension to your life. Blogging started purely as a hobby for him. It may now provide him with security and income in the future.

Louis' day job is director of corporate marketing for a high-performance network storage provider. In this role he uses traditional media to create a relationship with journalists and analysts. At the beginning of 2006 Louis created his blog – www.louisgray.com – to write about the world of Silicon Valley and web technologies, including social media, and his love of what he was discovering each day. He never set out to be visible; it was purely a hobby, sharing what he was learning.

Now, in 2009, Louis writes two blog posts a day. He writes them like an e-mail, a chat, a conversation, adding links and images. Each blog takes him only twenty minutes to write.

The majority of the time needed to create his blog is finding information to write about. At least three times a day Louis reads the feeds he receives through Google Reader.

Reading was the most time-consuming and enjoyable part of this process. He set up feeds and used the technology available to enable him to receive information from people and sites that he respected. At the beginning he didn't aim to create 'breaking news', he was commenting and observing on the industry. Every day he adds to his blog and increasingly he sees people subscribing to it.

Louis has become very connected to the source of the industry. Purely by being part of an ecosystem of like-minded people he hears of sites that had not been widely discovered and he contacts the developers of these sites and asks them if they would like his feedback or any other help he can provide. This was not for monetary gain. Louis' integrity as a writer and observer is of utmost importance.

In April 2008, Louis launched through his blog the start-up company, Socialmedian, a new site that he discovered that went on to enormous success for the founder, Jason Goldberg. Jason sold Socialmedian less than a year later to Xing, a German-based business network for $7.5 million. Louis was also the first person to write about TweetDeck (a utility to manage your Twitter network) on his blog. He was also among the first to adopt and evangelize FriendFeed.

Louis started his blogging life writing personal stuff, but quickly he saw the benefits of creating a brand and a niche and he is now recognized globally as one of the top bloggers among his peers. I asked Louis whether he had ever been approached by a company to write about them, a company that sees Louis as a great person to endorse them. He advised me that this is one of the occupational hazards of the brand he has created. If Louis writes about a new company it gives them a tremendous amount of credibility and visibility. However, Louis stressed that he would never write about a company for direct financial gain. The damage to his reputation would be enormous and trust would be lost. This is a critical point for anyone on the internet; trust and integrity must never be sold. Once lost it cannot be won back and the audience of fans would disappear in an instant. The viral nature of the internet spreads the word very quickly.

Louis did advise me that some companies have thanked him after he has written about them totally out of the blue. He has started acting as an official adviser to some companies, the equivalent of being given 'one per cent of a company worth zero'. I am happy with this. Louis is having an opportunity to create a pension for his family. A by-product of his contribution may be financial gain. To me this is justified and right, but remember it is not his reason for sharing or contributing.

Louis is an excellent example of someone who is gaining a 'know me' status on the internet. He has great visibility and his brand is trusted and liked, his blog is being advocated and 'twittered' all the time. Louis' network of followers is loyal and his followers have large networks. He is an example of someone who uses his blog as the centre of his activities. All other feeds and networks are there to serve him for information and knowledge.

An alternative example to learn from is through examining the way one individual is utilizing YouTube as their main focus. It is getting them 'known' and serving them in a different way to having a blog.

SHARING YOUR EXPERTISE THROUGH VIDEO

Mark Sinclair, a New Zealander based in the UK, is co-founder of www.yourbusinesschannel.com (yBC). Mark allowed me to discover how he leverages YouTube to enable his business to be visible and in turn is optimizing experts on search engines.

In 2004, Mark and his business partner James Kirk could see an opportunity to supply high-quality information to small businesses from experts using video, including leveraging YouTube as a community. The yBC team has now created over 600 shows, providing free advice to small businesses, utilizing experts from around the world. The model for this is a win-win. Mark is leveraging the experts and their knowledge, and the experts are leveraging Mark's ability to create followers to their knowledge on YouTube through his channel.

Found through searching Google, YouTube, other key video platforms, iTunes or being embedded inside experts' blogs or websites, these experts are having an opportunity to 'be known', while at the same time yBC, Mark's company, is gaining traffic and creating income through syndicating with partners across the world. Newspaper sites, blog owners and niche communities love having expert videos on their sites to provide great advice from leading-edge experts and show that they are embedding Web 2.0 tools in their websites.

Mark has created a channel for his experts inside YouTube, http://www.youtube.com/user/yourBusinessChannel. By running all his expert videos through this channel, Mark can create visibility and a cohesive message. This channel also enables him to start creating a community, with the ability for members of YouTube to subscribe to his channel for updates and comment on videos. Similar channels exist on other popular video platforms such as MySpace Video and MSN Video.

Mark's ability to create a viral marketing campaign around the videos is part of the genius of what he is doing. Those people who want to be associated with the experts he has filmed can embed the videos easily in their blogs and profiles. YouTube make it very easy to embed videos, encouraging the sharing of knowledge with others.

There is a great deal of similarity between Mark and Louis. Both are providing leading-edge content, one using blogs, the other using video and YouTube. Both are creating a 'know me' presence on the internet, with a wide base of people trusting in them due to their determination to only provide high-quality information that helps others. What we discover in the next chapter is how they use their 'like me' networks as places to achieve depth and they utilize these for knowledge and content, not for marketing.

I have shared with you information about two of the people I most admire within the world of social media. They have created blogs and videos that fully leverage social media and in doing this are also helping others to learn the subject. They are walking their talk and creating the noise that we all need to hear.

BLOGGING – GETTING STARTED

Remember, getting known is the first step in creating your brand, building trust and sharing your knowledge; it is in effect your marketing. 'Know me' focuses on you, it is about your knowledge, your connections and your links. It is about understanding how to leverage the social media and networking sites, it is about telling a lot of people what matters to you. It starts with you, but of course, you know that you can only be successful if what you are doing and saying is contributing to the knowledge and lives of others.

During my research for this book I came across Roger Knight, through his blog http://www.happyandprosperous.com. You may remember Roger's blog led me to the quote about 'drains and radiators' in Chapter four. I contacted Roger to ask him some questions about why he ran a blog. Roger is a homeopath and also has a website under his name, www.rogerknight.info. I have chosen Roger for you to learn from as he is not a social media guru, he is a normal man, with great intentions. Roger's website clearly states that he is a homeopath in Leeds and it is explicit about what he sells, in effect how he earns his money. You would expect this. Roger's blog, however, is much wider in its intention than his website and on it he states: 'Helping us all improve our lives person-ally and financially. The Best Is Yet To Come.' This indicated to me that Roger has much to contribute and offer, he is providing and sharing thoughts that he hopes will help others.

When I interviewed Roger I wanted to learn how having a blog helped him and whether this was part of an overall social media strategy.

ROGER'S STORY

Roger had started his blog as a way to attract clients and he was fairly underwhelmed by its success. In fact he was worried that he would not be a great case study for me, which is very considerate, but he could not be more wrong! What I learned from Roger will be able to help you understand that a blog cannot be done in isolation, it has to be connected in some way to communities and where the traffic is. A great phrase is 'fish where the fish are' and your blog is a great example of this.

Roger started his blog in October 2007 and to begin with he blogged every day, then he reduced this to once a week. Finally, he lost interest as he felt he was spending too much time for the rewards achieved. This is a shame, as I felt that Roger had enjoyed sharing his inspiring thoughts.

In addition to his blog he was spending time on www.stumbleupon.com to encourage visitors. This is a community of people that share recommendations of good sites to like-minded people. Its aim is to help you discover great sites that your friends recommend and, hopefully, you will become one of those 'great sites'.

Roger was also using www.mybloglog.com to track information about his traffic. Through this he learned who his blogs were being read by.

LEARNING HOW TO MAKE YOUR BLOG WORK FOR YOU

Let's look at what a blog is. A blog is much the same as an article you may have written to share your thoughts in a local paper, but now, it is global and can be found randomly. A blog also works well when others are adding their thoughts as comments. This is a sign that you have created a spark of interest and often the content added is just as interesting as the blog that was carefully authored. When you receive comments you are collecting like-minded people into your network, which is very powerful. You are creating followers.

Roger's content in his blogs is gentle and inspiring, a wide audience can enjoy them and in fact he said that most of his audience is in the USA, which he felt was not relevant for his business.

The obvious aspect of the internet is that you cannot

determine who will read your blogs or where the readers will be located, so you have three choices:

1. Enjoy your expanding, global network and see where those connections could lead your business and ideas.
2. Create a product or service that can be delivered globally.
3. Find a way of getting your blog into local people's view – create a local network online that will get to 'know you, like you, follow you'.

One aspect of today's business landscape is that we have to consider it as one world, with few geographical and even political and trading barriers. This requires you to make some strategic decisions and to keep your ear very close to the ground. Could Roger find a way, which suits his values and ethics, to deliver homeopathy advice that allows his trusted network across the world to buy from him?

A further learning point was the relevance of Roger's articles. Roger writes widely about topics that interest and inspire him. However, when I asked him who his clients typically are, it was clear that he was not writing relevant content around the type of people that would naturally want to utilize his skills.

Roger's clients are:

- 80% female
- Mostly over thirty
- Have skin or menstrual problems
- Those over forty concerned about menopause
- Some experience stress and this results in Irritable Bowel Syndrome
- Depression and anxiety are commonly discussed ailments.

Roger knew how to help people with these conditions and had a lot of experience and case studies that displayed his credibility and also his passion in this.

Roger's blog reflected that he wanted people to be happy and as a result achieve prosperity. He knew that the above ailments could stop a woman from achieving the life she wanted and deserved. His intentions were perfect and I have no doubt that, like me, many thousands of females have been inspired by Roger, but like me, they were not reading some of the relevant content that could actually enable them to either go and see him for help or refer him to a friend who would benefit from seeing him.

Roger discussed some thoughts with me and it was agreed that he could write about the conditions that he could help with and I was excited by this. A woman who was going through the menopause would probably want to read a blog about this when she googled for help; this would be of tremendous value. There is nothing more off-putting then just seeing adverts for pills when you google for help. A sympathetic article that guided them to a solution would be perfect.

Although I completely believe in the randomness and serendipitous nature of the internet, I also feel that you can increase your opportunity for success if you begin by 'fishing where the fish are'.

The great thing about a blog written for a particular condition or problem, be it health, stress, credit problems, lack of sales, marital difficulties, teenage children, the list goes on, is that people are emotional about their problems and will look for like-minded people who have these issues and can share and support.

THE POWER OF BLOGGING INSIDE COMMUNITIES

Through the use of Wordpress and Blogger, two very powerful blogging utilities, you can create your own blog. I have created one – www.pennypower.co.uk – on Wordpress. This blog enables me to have my own look and feel, but it is not a place where I have conversation, it is more about my visibility and the sharing of knowledge. The downside of creating your own blog is that you have to create the traffic to it. Much the same as the early days of e-commerce, blogging became the way to share your thoughts as opposed to sell your goods; each can be isolated if left outside of a community. This is why many companies have set up their 'stall' inside eBay to sell their goods. I liken this to having a counter inside a department store while you build your brand. Blogging is the same; you need a community around you. Creating a flow of visitors to your blog can be a challenge, so think of having a blog inside a community akin to having an article in the most-read newspaper or magazine.

Niche communities are a great way to attract like-minded people to you, a place where your content may be more relevant and where there are visitors 'passing by' who will see your blog as they randomly read and take part in the community. Let's look at the Ecademy community – a business community serving small businesses.

Ecademy serves, predominantly, business owners. From a survey conducted in February 2009 by Contact MCI, a marketing and consultancy company, I can extract these statistics. The number who answered this survey in a six-day period was over 3,000.

- 72% are male
- 63% call themselves 'self-employed'

- 84% say they use Ecademy via a laptop or home PC
- 61% are over forty-five years of age
- 50% refer to themselves as 'professionals', indicating they are consultants or accountants, lawyers, etc.

While this indicates that there are a lot of experienced and talented people in the community, it also reflects that they may all have similar pressures and worries. We can assume that many will have teenage children and it's likely that some will be having health issues. In Roger's case, of the 72 per cent of men, we can assume that many will have wives going through menopause. Those that work at home will suffer periods of isolation. Being self-employed they may have moments of doubt about their business and have self-worth issues.

This level of 'relevance' enables people to also see what services they can discuss and share. It is possible when you know this information to write blogs that will 'hit the nail on the head' and create conversation and advocacy.

I suggested to Roger that if he began to write blogs inside Ecademy and other communities that had his potential audience, then perhaps his return would be greater.

I am thrilled to report that Roger has joined Ecademy.[46] Roger is beginning his journey of being connected into a community. It started the day he joined and created his profile.

Sadly, there is a graveyard of profiles that have been created and then nothing else done. I hear people say 'I am a member of X community and it has made no difference to my business.' I am sorry to say that it is a poor workman that blames his tools. You have to be active inside the networks and contribute. Without activities how can you actually be noticed or create fans, followers and prospects?

A great analogy is when people join a health club to lose

weight at the beginning of the year. New Year's resolutions, they are tough! Halfway through the year they have not been back since the first visit and they are, of course, still overweight and lacking energy. They can't blame the health club, can they?

Later on I am going to cover the power of advocates, or as some call them 'ambassadors'. For now I want to touch on this to explain a further learning point for Roger.

Blogging gives you an opportunity to create friendships and advocates that will support and share in your dreams, passions and goals. There are many famous bloggers that have created a base of friends, fans and advocates that keep their dream alive and constantly pass on their blogs to people who could enjoy their content. The viral nature of blogging cannot be underestimated. Last night my sixteen-year-old daughter said 'the internet makes dreams happen'. This is an interesting perspective from a young person. We then went on to discuss the fact that the internet is at such an early stage. I explained what TV was like when I was her age and how far it has come. The internet will be so different in thirty years, but the people and the dreams will remain the same.

So writing blogs can help to make your dreams materialize and if you write with enough frequency you become an online columnist. I bet you have a favourite columnist in your newspaper or magazine that you look out for when you get a chance to sit down and read a hard-copy newspaper? Writing one blog in isolation will not create success long term. It may create a short-term result immediately, but what you want is long-term momentum and audience retention.

When I look at the blog area on Ecademy I can see a list of log headings, titles that may inspire you, then I see a number alongside that tells me how many views the blog has received and how many comments have been added. The 'view count' indicates that the heading attracted a number of people to open the blog. The number of 'comments' indicates how many people were inspired to contribute to the discussion or provide advice. Never underestimate the 'lurkers'. They are absorbing what you say and may even advocate the blog on. the lurkers are your audience, while those that comment are your contributors.

I have an example of a lady called Lizzi Vandorpe, who wrote a blog on 4 December 2008.[47] It was her third blog on Ecademy. She has now gone on to be a prolific blogger and member of the community. Her blog was titled 'The Blessings Book Concept' and was about the creation of her idea to help people count their blessings.[48] I have to say that I have bought ten of these books for friends and family!

In Lizzi's blog her first contributor was a homeopath in England, called Linda Lloyd.[49] This is what Linda said in her comment:

Hi Elizabeth,
I thought I'd let you know that I visited your Blessings Book website earlier today. Just goes to show what can happen when you come from the heart.

I've kept a 'Gratitude Journal' for some years myself, I love re-reading it and remembering and enjoying things that made me happy, some big and some small.

What I really liked was the rose quartz crystal hearts you are selling at a really good price, because you are giving 100 per cent of the purchase price to a monthly charity.

I liked the idea so much that I've included the details and a link to that page in my up-coming news-letter, which goes out to about 900 people. I thought I'd just let them know they could buy a lovely token

for a special person or a really unusual stocking-filler –
and give to charity at the same time.

I hope this is okay with you – the newsletter hasn't
gone out yet so let me know.

OK with Lizzi? My goodness, that is just incredible. Her book
was only due out that month and already she had an advocate
in Linda who had e-mailed 900 people. Lizzi had been
distributed to 900 new contacts. What is also interesting is
that Lizzi is selling rose quartz crystal hearts; these were not
even mentioned in her blog but it was these that inspired
Linda to take action. Life online is random and unstructured
and you cannot control the outcome! I contacted Lizzi and
Linda to ask if I could include them in my book. Twelve
hours later I saw this on Twitter from Linda:

> Penny Power of Ecademy is writing a book and
> quoting me as an example of what friends and
> advocates can do for your business :)

Are you starting to see the links and the significance? That
twitter achieved two things; the first is that it elevated Linda
as a person who advocates and helps others, the second is that
it mentioned me and my book, teasing the market in such a
subtle way that creates a buzz, but is not self-promoting.

FOUR TIPS FOR GREAT BLOGGING

In addition to the thoughts above here are some tips.

1. Blog regularly, provide good content and share knowledge. Don't sell!

It is absolutely fatal to your reputation if you sell in a blog. These are called 'blogverts', a cross between a blog and an advert. Remember, I have stressed throughout that self-promotion is not good. You can get a great following if you are genuine and you show that you want to teach and help. Success is a by-product of what you do. Do not target it as you cannot and will not win. Google also despises this, as when someone searches on Google for information, they want their users to gain knowledge not to be sold to unless they clicked on a Google ad.

2. Consider a great heading for your blog

I find that blog headings that are written as a question inspire participation. A quick glance at the twenty most recent blogs on Ecademy show me that six of them are questions and those six have the greatest level of participation. It is easy to understand because a question is conversational, a heading without one is more like a statement or a broadcast. Remember, conversation is good!

I was once sent a sample blog by a member who wanted advice. She was promoting a health and well-being expert. It was two pages of information about him and it was so boring, unless of course you had decided you wanted to read his biography! This would require a seriously targeted approach, random would not come into your marketing plan! I suggested that instead of this 'masterpiece' perhaps a short blog like this would work:

How do you stay well?
I am interested in talking to business owners on
Ecademy that have managed to stay healthy and well,
despite the pressures of family, work, money and
stress.

I represent a well-being therapist and we are always
wanting to learn about and empathize with entrepreneurs and the pressure they are under. If you can
share your thoughts here that would be great. If you
prefer to be private, please send me a message.

This type of blog gives others an opportunity to talk, to share
their stories. Those that don't want to share openly may
contact you directly or may just enjoy finding comfort and
inspiration in the discussion that takes place.

What is important here is that you are creating a following
and a brand around your intention.

3. Encourage and get involved in the conversation

Don't start a conversation and then walk away, this would be
rude in any context. Can you imagine doing that at a bar with
some friends? It would be ridiculous. Make sure that you
participate in the discussion, but don't get personal if they
disagree with your point of view!

I have witnessed people taking their blog down because
they didn't like someone challenging their thoughts.
Providing everyone remains polite, constructive and keeps to
the discussion, all is fine and you should welcome opinions. It
is really bad ethics to take down a blog unless there is a
serious reason. You don't own the content that they write and
when they contribute they are using their time and energy
and you cannot control them in this way.

There are some occasions when you can take action if

things are not good on your blog. On Ecademy we have a feedback tab on everyone's profile that notifies our best practice team. On other sites you may need to contact the support team, usually e-mailed as support@companyname.com.

Don't put up with the following:

- Blog hijacking – this is when someone spams irrelevant content on your blog.
- Swearing or abuse – ensure that the content is something you are happy to be represented by. While they are damaging themselves more than you, you don't want to have this on your blog.

If any of these things happen, gently try to bring the conversation back in line or ask someone in your close network to help you. Do not get involved in public slanging matches or do anything that is against your core values. It can be tempting, but don't!

4. Optimization of your blog

One of the advantages of blogging in a busy community is the optimization you will achieve on search engines like Google. This has become quite a frenzy and sadly some are blogging just to achieve this. Once again, your intentions will be obvious and no one likes that. Just be aware that what you write will be visible on search engines. This is a great benefit, providing you are happy that your blog represents you well.

TWITTER

I absolutely have to talk about Twitter in this section, as I do in all three areas of 'know me, like me, follow me', as Twitter is the ultimate way to create a wide network very quickly. I also talk about it in Chapter eight *Like me*, because it is a brilliant way to advocate others and in Chapter nine *Follow me*, as of course it is the perfect example of the behaviour 'follow'.

Twitter enables you to write up to 140 characters of information and 'tweet' it to your network of followers and into the public domain. Twitter is really part of building a wide network and is firmly in the 'know me' area. However, Twitter will become more sophisticated as the users become clearer about the way they use it. It is clearly random, open and unstructured and the day we saw it become a big player was the day that the management team on Ecademy celebrated. Twitter and Ecademy are the two networks that believe in this new world of being open, random and supportive.

Once you have your account you have the facility to write 140 characters into the 'home' area, saying 'what you are doing now'. This feature of telling the world what you are doing exists also in Facebook and Ecademy. It is a great way of sending out small, token thoughts and creating a vibration. This 'vibration' may be randomly picked up and as a result a new person might follow you or someone might just click on a link you have embedded in your 'tweet' and read it.

Where this becomes very interesting is when you start to look at people's profile updates and you can see who is contributing and following others and who is just broadcasting any noise.

The best way to get followers and build a presence is to ensure that wherever you are inside social media you have a way of linking people to your 'follow me' profile on Twitter. There is even a site called www.twitterbuttons.com, where you can add your Twitter name and they will provide you with a great image and the embed code to enable you to add this to your blog, profile, website, etc. I really encourage you to do this as the easier you make it to create a wide network the better.

QUANTITY, QUALITY AND DIRECTION

In the mid-1980s, when I was in sales for an IT company, I met Nicole Wehden, a very special person who has remained a part of my life ever since.[50] Nicole now runs a highly success-ful community site that encourages people to do favours for each other by swapping skills – www.swapaskill.com.

Nicole taught me a process that she learnt when working for a training company called Mercuri International.[51] It was called Quantity, Quality and Direction. This process is simple and can be applied so well to what I have talked about in this section. It is important with anything you do to:

- Be active – Quantity
- Share your knowledge well – Quality
- Spend time attracting the right audience – Direction

Imagine two of these without the other!

QUALITY AND QUANTITY BUT NO DIRECTION

I like to spend time writing great blogs and do this regularly. Those that contact me are very good but not enough people seem to see them.

This person takes time over their content and is good at

writing blogs, the quality of their blogs is fine, they also write regularly, finding interesting things to say about their expertise and industry. So they are clearly spending time on this each week; however, their weakness is that they are not ensuring that the people who would benefit from seeing their blogs are reading them. They are not creating links or placing the blog in the right places. They have yet to sort out where to direct their content.

QUANTITY AND DIRECTION BUT NOT HIGH ENOUGH QUALITY

I spend all my time in one social network and blog a lot. I know that I am attracting the right people, but I don't seem to create advocates, followers or customers.

This person seems to be doing enough activity and is focused on a social network where the relevance is right, but they may be writing too many blogs for the level of knowledge they have, which can weaken their credibility. Be wary of blogging just for visibility.

QUALITY AND DIRECTION – BUT NOT REGULAR ENOUGH TO FORM TRUST AND VISIBILITY

I like to spend a lot of time writing my blog. I worry about how good it is. I think it is like public speaking so feel exposed. I am also committed to a small network and have a lot of depth in it. I feel safe when I know the people well. I am not achieving a lot of success from my blogging, so I don't do it very often.

This is a very common example of how people feel about blogging and it is limited because they are fearful of quantity and the random nature of being highly visible. I have empathy with this concern but at the same time regular visibility is important. Creating fresh content to keep people interested and connecting with you is critical. It is very off-putting when content is old and when people look at your profile and see that you haven't updated content recently.

Thankfully, social media is becoming easier. Blogging is time-consuming and this has given rise to micro-blogging or SMS on the internet. Twitter is very popular now and this is a way of writing only 140 characters and still being visible and credible. It is important not to rely on Twitter though, as much of the tweeting on Twitter is links to great blogs and content that people see and want to pass on. You want to be one of those great bloggers too!

LEAP OF FAITH

My final note on blogging is to trust me and take a leap of faith. You will not know what can be achieved until you do this. Joining a community that has the blogging tools will help you to do this in a gentle way. Having your own blog on Wordpress[52] or Blogger[53] is a bigger step, but you may decide it is a good one.

BENEFITS OF A WIDE NETWORK

'Know me' is your first step into creating you and your organization's online brand and reputation. Being known will attract people to you if you are active, knowledgeable and have the right transparent intention. You will have to accept the random nature of building a wide network and not judge who wants to know you.

The successful people building a 'know me' network also understand that to become known you have to be liked and trusted. A weak brand will soon be discovered. Sadly, I know of many people who can create a lot of noise but have little substance to back it up. 'Know me' is just the start, but the next phase of building network value is 'like me'. 'Like me' is critical as this is where you will create the depth and the foundations to sustain yourself, build your knowledge and, critically, be advocated.

In the next chapter we will learn about people that understand the importance of being liked, and it is by being liked that their network has grown in quality and relevance.

CHAPTER 8

LIKE ME – CREATING YOUR SOCIAL NETWORKING FOOTPRINT

THE PREVIOUS CHAPTER covered the importance of building a wide network of people who will be aware of you and know you exist. They may read your blogs, see your videos or notice your contribution in groups and on Twitter. The upside of 'know me' is that it is about using the technology to distribute your thoughts and knowledge. It is more like a broadcast so it is easier to take on board and execute if you are a task-oriented person.

The downside of staying in 'know me' all the time is that people won't know you well enough to really trust you and to know what help they can give you. It is easy to be a closed person if you stay in the 'know me area' all the time, you don't have to reveal much about yourself. 'Know me' is more about 'what you are' whereas 'like me' is much more about 'who you are'. 'Like me' is about leveraging the social networks and creating depth in your network. Here you will create followers who will have conversations with you. 'Like me' is about 'sharing and collecting people'.

WHO ARE YOU?

Who you are encompasses the whole you, not just your knowledge, skills and the way you make your money. It is about things that matter to you – your family, where you go on holiday, which causes you support. It is also about the journey you have had in life that has enabled you to be the expert you are. It is about why you like what you do.

In this chapter I want you to think in broader terms than marketing. Your business is about you. People will work with you because they like and trust you; they will talk about you if you are reliable, caring and help others. This is about your integrity, your values, your friendship and your ability to be part of a community.

Ecademy features in this chapter as it is the site I know best that has its focus on community. While it provides tools for visibility and marketing yourself, its most powerful aspect, unique to Ecademy in the online business networks, is its sense of community.

'Like me' is about taking your connections to a deeper level; it is about building depth in your network by revealing yourself and being interested in others. While 'know me' is about width, 'like me' is about depth in your network.

THE PLAYGROUND TRAP

This scenario makes me think back to the first seven years of being a mum. I went to the same playground for five years to collect my children from their infant school.

I was well known. I ran the parents' group for a while, I helped in school listening to children read and I knew most of the mums in the playground at pick-up time. 'Networking for mummies', it was wonderful, often my sanity. There were about 100 mums at the school. I knew each one as 'Jack's mum', 'Emily's mum', and they knew me as 'Hannah, Ross or TJ's mum'. The amazing thing is that we were familiar with one another, but in many cases we knew nothing about each other. I could have been about to buy a new conservatory for our garden and the 'mum' next to me in the playground could be the best supplier for that, but our conversations never actually moved on to what we did for a living. We stayed in another world of familiarity around the subject we had in common, children.

I see this a great deal when I go to networking events. People share a laugh, talk about their day and get so used to chatting at a certain level that they forget to ask, or perhaps are too embarrassed to ask, 'I am sorry, I forgot, what is it that you do for a living?' People's lives move on and what they did when you first met them may have changed, or your needs may have changed, and what they do now could be exactly the knowledge you need.

This is why it is very important to combine 'know me' and 'like me' in your marketing. 'Know me' reminds people what you do, 'like me' continues to build the trust and the bond.

I said that 'know me' is about using the technology, in effect the tools/utilities that social media provides – it is about 'using'. 'Like me' is about community, about becoming a member in a community where your reputation can spread. It is about 'belonging'.

LIKE ME BECAUSE OF WHO I AM

'Like me' is about you, who you are. This is tough to teach as it is about being one of those people who stand out from the crowd, it not something you can force. 'You have to like me' is not a sentence we can pass on! Whereas 'know me' is like a broadcast, 'like me' is a feeling, a sentiment, an emotion that only you can create and that most certainly cannot be achieved unless you are willing to contribute and help others.

I guess 'like me' is a time-consuming aspect of building your profile, but equally it is very rewarding. The feedback and support you receive feeds your self-esteem and your self-belief. I often imagine our members coming in from a tough day out 'selling' and having moments of self-doubt and then receiving a wonderful testimonial from a member they helped or reading some comments on a blog they wrote and feeling that sense of belonging and appreciation that was lacking when you were out trying to win business. Working alone or in a small business is not easy. It can be fulfilling, but it can be lonely and isolating, and if you stay in 'broadcast mode' you will severely lack the emotional support that we all need from time to time.

DOES 'KNOW ME' HAVE TO BE FIRST?

One of the most amazing aspects of this new world is the ability for anyone to start a business and take responsibility for their income and future. The independent worker, the homeworker, being self-employed, the individual capitalist – take your pick, this can be or is already you. I have seen so many amazing people start their businesses on Ecademy and find their suppliers and their customers all from one community and one website. To me that is simply awesome, and what those people have in common is that they have embedded themselves in the community. They have started with the need to be liked and to like people and from that place of confidence they have then moved into 'know me'. So it is possible to build a deep network before you build a wide one. In fact, I would say that many people choose this route first. This does not mean we have to turn the process on its head. 'Know me' will become the starting point in your marketing strategy once you have built confidence and had some encouraging conversations.

'Like me' is your 'conversation marketing', it is the exchange of private messages, it is the offline meeting where you sit and chat to one person and start to build a business friendship with them.

COMMUNITY FIRST!

There is a wonderful member of Ecademy in India called Abha Banerjee, who was recently named India's first Woman Motivational Speaker.[54] Abha is a vibrant, energetic and warm person. I had the pleasure of meeting Abha when I was touring Southeast Asia meeting members in 2005. Abha joined Ecademy in 2004 after she had decided to follow her dream of being a speaker to motivate others to make changes in their lives.

In 2004, Ecademy was very focused on community. In fact that was the most critical part at that time due to the lack of Web 2.0 tools: they came along later. This is one of the reasons Ecademy is such a strong community. In 1998 when we started, community was the main application! Blogging and other 'visibility' tools had not yet been created, so community was always the focus. This is what sets Ecademy apart from the pack, 'community first – commerce second' has always been our belief and foundation.

In the previous chapter I covered blogging and YouTube

as ways to be known. In this chapter I will cover community, as it is only by being part of a community that you will be able to achieve the 'like me' level, critical for the development of you and your business.

I am going to tell you Abha's story as it represents many who have seen the power of community and have developed a deep, strong network that has helped them far beyond just being visible. Abha does not see Ecademy as her marketing tool; it is her family and her home. As a result of the way Abha has contributed and cared for her fellow members in the community, Abha has seen her life and business develop. I think all readers will identify with Abha and the journey she is on.

ABHA'S STORY

In 2004 when Abha joined Ecademy she had decided to stop being a lawyer and pursue her dream of becoming a life coach and a speaker. She felt a bit isolated and alone having moved on from full-time legal practice to delve into a totally new field, training to be a life coach. Feeling the need to retrain herself, to find requisite resources and to help her face a world amused by her decision, she came into Ecademy hoping to simply network to build her new business.

Abha said, 'Like every other dreamer I faced ridicule, rejection and scepticism from people close to me from my old business world.' This is a common experience for many people embarking on a new way of living and working. Sometimes it is tough for those close to them to see the new person that is emerging. 'As if to lift me out of confused emotions and negative feelings, Ecademy entered my life as the non-judgemental listener.' What a wonderful interpretation of how the people inside the community helped Abha.

Before Abha joined Ecademy she had only ever used Google and e-mail, she had not experienced social networking. She began by creating a basic profile, added a photo and started to connect slowly with a few people. Getting to know people and letting them get to know her was inspiring and it took her into a world that was far beyond India, making friends and learning from people all across the world. This gave Abha strength and determination and answered many of her questions that she had each day. In time, Abha found that she was answering people's questions and helping them. At the beginning she was being given advice and listening to others and now she was the one giving the advice and others were listening to her. This was very empowering for Abha and she realized Ecademy was more than a networking platform, it was like your very own personal support system, where you have an opportunity to share your beliefs and the community comes forwards to support and stand by you. People's responses and communication became a source of personal discovery for her and she kept adding to herself as a person. Over time Abha received many testimonials from people, providing her with visibility and credibility.

Abha had not set out to build a brand on Ecademy, but because of what she communicated through her profile she started to see that she was being advocated as an ideas person with good intentions and integrity. These testimonials added to Abha's brand and her personal presence. Thanks to the very affectionate and powerful feedback that people sent to Abha, she realized that she should develop her personal brand. This was another very effective and positive aspect of being in a vibrant, thinking and pro-active community. Based on the feedback, her decision was reaffirmed and Abha knew that the switch from being a lawyer to a life coach would work, and her desire to inspire and motivate would ensure it.

Ecademy acted as a very strong, live and real feedback system for Abha. She learned at this point that her personal brand was far more critical than her 'corporate brand'. In the midst of thousands of speakers and coaches, Abha needed to stand out as an individual. She then realized the power of having advocates and supporters who would tell others about her, people who knew and trusted her and critically, people who liked her.

Abha achieved all of this while at home, on her PC, not leaving her house, still helping her kids with their homework, still 'watching her daughter suck her feet' – a beautiful image that Abha conjures up of being a mum. This dimension of Abha's life is such an important aspect of social networking online. So much can be achieved for little cost and no destruction of your family's needs and values.

In time Abha began to write blogs, submit articles to other websites and run groups. She learnt to do all these while on Ecademy, something she had never delved into before. This continued to build her brand and provided Abha with the knowledge and expertise to ensure she built her credibility. Over a couple of years Abha found herself becoming a certified life coach, a professional speaker, an expert in emotional intelligence and personal leadership and was named one of the Top Ten Life and Business Success Coaches in Asia.

While Abha continued to train herself and gain recognition, she shared her progress and successes with her friends on Ecademy who had been with Abha throughout her journey, in the same way she shared theirs. They found it comfortable to advocate for her and talk about her as a brand. Abha stressed that she 'could reach people that would have been impossible to reach across the world, because

Ecademy gives you an opportunity to go public in a safe environment'.

Abha's story of discovering her value and how she could leverage it is inspiring but not unique. We find ourselves in others if we take time to talk and listen. We think we have all the answers, and we do, but sometimes the answers are buried deep inside us and they have to be coaxed out through the conversations we have with others.

You don't need to know the direction you are heading in all the time. In fact, the most powerful aspect of being part of a community and building depth within your network is that ideas flow towards you and you will hear and witness the needs of others. Each of us is tuned to hear different things and that is how we create our unique offering and create our unique brands.

BE ALERT TO PEOPLE – TRUST HAS TO BE EARNED

Abha built her deep network of advocates and friends across the world online. Online you can meet so many people in such a short space of time without leaving your home. Trust has to be earned though. Be alert to the downside of the internet. It is impossible to be 100 per cent sure of the person you are talking to, so always get to know what others are saying about people and the reputation they have. Nothing replaces offline for being totally sure that people are real and not pretending to be something they are not. Being inside a community helps to protect you from people who are posing as someone else, so make sure you utilize your network to ensure the authenticity of anyone before you become close enough to open up and reveal your needs or weaknesses and before you trade. This is where 'what people say about you' is so powerful. Trust is critical and you have to earn trust, it cannot be bought or broadcast.

Ecademy has always verified the subscribing members via their credit card transactions. Twitter is now offering verification. This is an activity that we will see increasingly on the internet to ensure trust.

MEETING PEOPLE

One of the distinct weaknesses of the social media world is that many sites fail to encourage meeting one another face to face. You will remember that for Thomas, meeting people is the most important aspect of social media. He leverages social media to ultimately find people that he wants to meet and this is one of the reasons that Ecademy has ensured that we have an events tool and over 500 meetings are organized by members across the world every month. This need was also confirmed when I interviewed Chuck Zdrojowy, based in Atlanta, USA.[55]

Chuck is a specialist in supply chain management. As a consultant he discovered social networking in 2006. He decided to create 'hubs' within Ning. In Ning's words, 'Ning lets you create new social experiences for the most important people and interests in your life.' It is a place where you can create your own social network. After two years Chuck had 4,000 members in his clubs. He then looked around for other networks that would allow him to build networks of people around him that could meet locally. He found Ecademy.

Chuck was attracted to Ecademy because of the sense of community around small business owners and the fact that there was an events area where members could create clubs and then invite and publicize events locally. To Chuck, social media is most useful for him as a way of meeting people. Chuck is interested in the depth of relationships and wants to be part of a community that encourages this.

Chuck now runs Link Atlanta, a group inside Ecademy that meets and helps one another locally. His network is made up of people who are comfortable networking offline but the online world is confusing and scary to many of them. Chuck has now created a training course called www.learn2linkonline.com. The goal for Chuck through his course is to help individuals and small- to medium-sized businesses develop and execute their social media strategy.

Chuck is embedded inside social media with his brand being about linking people together in Atlanta. He has his Twitter account – 'link_atlanta', his own social network on Ning – http://linkatlanta.ning.com/ and his Link Atlanta Group on Ecademy. According to Chuck 'social media is my enabler to meet new people online and ultimately offline'.

Building trust is about getting to know people well and moving the person from purely knowing you exist to liking you. Later, I will share with you some case studies of how experts are using sites such as Socialmedian and FriendFeed to build a deep network. Their reason for this is purely for knowledge. This is where they build trust because of the knowledge they share. Few people are using these sites for their marketing, for them this is only about collaboration and sharing knowledge for the greater good.

In May 2009, Thomas launched offline walking with your network while learning about Twitter. Twalkes are becoming popular worldwide now – an inspiration that indicates people want to meet up.

ADVOCACY

The greatest aspect of 'like me' is the power of creating advocates around your knowledge, people who will 'talk about you when you are not in the room'. To me this is real network value. 'Know me' cannot achieve this. People may say, 'that guy who writes about health may be a good person to get in touch with', but it is far more powerful if they are able to say, 'I know James, he is a really good man, I know that he cares deeply about people's well-being and he is a trustworthy man who will really look after you.' You cannot achieve the second accolade without having a relationship with that advocate.

Advocacy in its purest form is the ability for a person to influence the outcome of a situation. When you have a strong relationship with others and they believe deeply in your ability, the power of their word can influence your life. Like having a sales force, advocates can feed you business.

Several years ago I was at an Ecademy event with the premium membership group called BlackStar. BlackStars on Ecademy pay a significantly higher fee to use the site as they have decided to commit as 'life members'. For this commitment they receive access to more powerful time-saving tools on the website and they meet monthly face to face to mentor, share and collaborate with one another. They get to know each other at a deeper level and build trust. The BlackStars pay more so are more serious at seeking out a higher return for their time and investment. This creates a highly productive, intimate network.

On this particular day in March 2007, the speaker was a much respected member of BlackStar called Dave Clarke.[56] Dave is the CEO of a lunchtime business network that meets in several cities around the UK every month. We strongly

recommend NRG http://www.nrg-networks.com to our
network in Ecademy.

Dave's talk was about his experience of being a BlackStar
and how he had achieved a significant growth in his business.
Dave was not an online guy, he liked the offline world and felt
comfortable in this place. He saw Ecademy as a way to meet
people, to build trust and get to know and like them. During
his talk Dave provided us with the following information,
starting with his philosophy:

> Business networking, for me, is about connecting with
> others, then building relationships with some of those.
> I then become an advocate for some of them. These
> are people I know, like, and trust *and* I promote them
> as a matter of course when I find an opportunity.

> - I have met 173 members at events.
> - I have followed up with a one-to-one interaction with
>   129 of those.
> - I have an ongoing business relationship at some level
>   with 84 of those.
> - I have become an advocate for 26 of them. In effect,
>   I have 26 other business people with me when I meet
>   with clients and other people in business.

After his talk I stood up and thanked him and then I put the
room on the spot. I asked if anyone in the room was an
advocate for Dave and his business and thirty-seven people
put their hands up. You could hear a pin drop. It was a very
humbling experience for us all. Dave knew at that moment
that he was not alone in his business, thirty-seven other
people were advocating and supporting him.

The statistics above from Dave were provided in March

2007. Dave's network has grown significantly since then. I know that since that time Dave has opened many new lunchtime networking clubs across the UK, most being run by people he has met in Ecademy, specifically within BlackStar. This means that Dave's business has grown not just in terms of the number of members joining his network, but also in its distribution across the UK. He has advocates who are now working with him in a formal way to build their life. Now many of his advocates are people he collaborates with too.

TWITTER

I am going to talk about Twitter here because I use Twitter as a way of advocating others and their content. The appeal of Twitter is the simple way that it can be used. The most amazing thing is that no one really knows how it works. It seems that the founders have created a great utility and the people inside are creating the community and finding a way for it to help them and help others. Everyone will use it differently. You will find the way that it works for you, but you need to dive in and get very wet, risk drowning and know that eventually you will find the stroke that suits you.

I see Twitter as my most important tool for advocating others, for ensuring that the people I follow and respect and like are being distributed out there.

Many sites now allow you to twitter a link from their site. On Ecademy, for example, I can read a blog that someone has written and if I like it and feel it fits with my intentions to help business owners learn and grow, then I will click on the twitter link on the blog page and immediately that link and the title of the blog will be 'twittered' across my network.

Twitter sits across the three aspects of 'know me, like me,

follow me' and it is how you use it that will determine whether you create a large network of people that know you, a conversational, advocating network of people you like or a way of creating a following that enables you to be re-tweeted and helps to spread your brand and knowledge.

I will talk more about how to measure your following in the next chapter.

COLLABORATION

Networking is not just about finding business, it is also about business development. This was very clear when I interviewed Abha. She developed her business and knowledge through her network and then she started to win clients. When you are in business your needs are wider than just the next order. You need to develop your knowledge, your processes, your time management, your self-esteem, your distribution and your financial management. You are a one-person corporation, you need to have access to the skills and knowledge of all the same things that a large organization does but it all rests on your shoulders and you do not have a team of staff to delegate to. This is when building a network of people that you can collaborate with is so powerful.

Earlier in this book I talked about the business model that we have adopted within Ecademy, a modern way of running and building a business that does not require offices or large numbers of staff. Glenn Watkins has built Ecademy as a low-cost, highly efficient global business. The costs of our business are associated with delivering a great service not property and human resources. This does not mean that people are not involved, of course they are. It just means that the business is not directly employing large numbers of people, meaning that the work being done is by specialists who focus on specific tasks and are awesome at them. Glenn is a master collaborator, he is a High Red in terms of his behaviour style. As a High Red, Glenn is interested in return on investment, is a brilliant manager of time and wants to know that he is working with people who are committed to the same goals. The profile of a leader is very often a High Red, someone who knows how to collaborate.

Creating collaborative teams inside communities is one of the most successful ways of leveraging a network that you like and trust. It is efficient and powerful and the momentum that can be created through the joining of minds, networks and knowledge when focused on a shared goal is what can make the difference between an average success and a huge one. I looked up collaboration on Wikipedia and these words shone from the screen: 'Collaboration is a recursive process where two or more people or organizations work together towards an intersection of common goals.'

COLLABORATING WITH YOUR COMPETITORS

One of the most interesting aspects of observing a global, open, random and supportive network like Ecademy is that I have seen many people who in the past would have seen each other as competitors and been very secretive and closed off about the way they work now working together to increase each others' abilities, networks and profiles. The sharing of knowledge and contacts has helped many people become more successful, especially when they are in the same industry and target similar clients.

Recently my father, Duff Ross, shared a story with me from when he was a soldier in Egypt in the late 1940s. The most powerful aspect of what he shared was that it was about how two people who were on opposite sides came together to solve a problem.

In 1946 my father was serving in Egypt as a patrol commander. His role was to protect the copper assets that were being stripped off communication wires by robbers stealing the copper to sell it for profit.

One night my father went out on patrol with a German prisoner of war (POW) as his driver to retrieve some copper communication cables that were being stolen from a cave. It was after the war but the German soldiers had not been repatriated back into their country. The 'prisoners' were being utilized as drivers. When they reached the cave, my father jumped out of the car and he looked across and saw that his colleague was frozen with fear, frightened of what might happen if they confronted the robbers. My father knew he could not do it on his own. As he looked across at the German POW he saw that he was prepared to help. My father passed him a gun and together they went in and supported one another and recovered the cables.

This is a wonderful story of understanding that collaboration is the key to success in many instances, providing that your goals are clear and each person knows what they can uniquely contribute.

To go alone through life, believing and trusting only yourself, can be isolating and also relies on your having too broad a set of skills. The world is accelerating at hyperspeed and keeping up is no longer something we can do in isolation. Trusting in others and learning what they can do to complement your strengths and weaknesses is the most successful and efficient way of building your business.

Being a good collaborator relies on having a set of beliefs that reflect two things:

1. You are interested in helping the person at the end of the project, it is not about you.
2. Trusting others to be as good as you or better!

These are tough to achieve if you are arrogant or a control freak! The first relies on your being interested only in the outcome for the person who you are focusing on; the second relies on your realizing that you cannot be everything to all people.

STOP CONTROLLING AND START SHARING

Ecademy has never set out to be all things to all people or to control and own a member exclusively. We have embraced all the networks and have promoted them all to our members. Our goal is that your business grows. If this means you need to spend time on other networks to achieve that then we are happy to help you. I have experienced many blocks from people who view us as competitors, traditional institutions who are fearful of promoting us to their members in case their members choose to change their loyalty to us. This will in the end be the demise of these institutions because they will lose trust and, critically, they will not learn the value that twenty-first-century business is pinned on – one of empowering the customer, not owning or controlling them.

The reverse of this attitude is when we interact and collaborate with BNI, the world's largest offline network. It is a breakfast network for business people and they have more than 5,400 breakfast meetings across the world every week. Ivan Misner, the founder of BNI, has actively encouraged his members to use Ecademy as their online network and Thomas and I have spoken at BNI events in Europe, Dubai,

India and Southeast Asia. I applaud and promote BNI for their complete focus on the success of their members. They are committed to helping businesses grow through their attitude of 'givers gain'. Together Ecademy and BNI are a successful partnership. We do not hold a contract between us and there is no formal agreement, we just know that working together works for our members and that is enough.

FINDING YOUR COLLABORATIVE PARTNERSHIPS

If you want to build momentum in your business and find a way of building your business beyond your personal skills, ability, knowledge and time, then collaboration will be the key to your success. Creating depth in your network and learning to know, like, trust and follow others and seeing the value of being known, liked, trusted and followed will open your world up to the possibilities.

William Buist is a member of Ecademy and a wonderful role model for others to learn from.[57] I want to share with you his values, goals and business model to help you see how this can work for you. I mentioned William earlier (see page 102). William is the guy who said 'the wider his network has grown the more efficient he has become'. William is very good at building depth in his network but he has also learnt to develop width as he has seen how this helps him to be more efficient and visible. As his business has grown he has become more efficient in managing his time and being able to embrace a large network has become part of his business strategy.

William is a business consultant and helps companies to improve their ability to collaborate either internally in their own teams or through their wider connections with suppliers and customers. He focuses on serving businesses, networks and communities with his knowledge and contacts.

When I met with William I asked him how he has developed his business beyond his own time and knowledge. William explained the following process to me, all leveraging from the network he has developed inside Ecademy:

1. **Build a wide network** 'I have built a large network so I can be focused. I believe in random connections and know that if I meet one hundred people online randomly I will find one connection that is perfect for my business; if I meet a thousand people I will find ten perfect matches.'

    To William it is a numbers game at the beginning; this is why he has learned that having a wide network works for him.

2. **Build a brand** 'I want to be known for the things I want to be known for. I am careful to contribute on topics that are relevant to my business in order to attract the right people to me. Building my brand is critical for this.'

    Your brand is defined by your activity, so William writes about advocacy, collaboration, networking and social media. He also runs several groups focused on debating, networking and collaboration.

3. **Look out for new business partners** 'I constantly look out for new partners for my business to support new clients that I bring into the business. When I find the right partner I then match them to the clients' needs and that broadens my appeal and my service offerings.'

    William keeps his ear to the ground, both with his clients to assess their needs and inside his network to hear who can service those newly discovered needs.

4. **Create a delivery team** 'I ensure I have the best delivery team around me to service my clients. They start off as a

supplier to me and if they pass that test they can become a partner and work with me helping my clients.'

William spends an increasing amount of his time managing the customer relationship and networking and less of his time delivering. He delivers only within the areas that he is the expert in, his 'partners' are specialized and add their unique value.

5. **Keep costs low** 'My fixed costs are my suppliers such as my PR, my PA and my graphic designer, my variable costs are those parts of my business that I can pass on and invoice to my clients. In this way I act as the middleman, always being the manager of the client relationship and taking full responsibility for their satisfaction.'

   William is a businessman who knows how to keep his costs low: minimal travel, no offices and no 'fat'. His business has few overheads and most of the costs are related to servicing the client.

6. **Create a trusted brand** within his area of expertise 'I have become the route to anything and everything for business. I can outsource most of the needs of my clients to my trusted close network. This is why having a large network is critical as I can find the best within that network. The best rise to the top of networks, the larger the network the better people have to be.'

   William knows that the most important asset for his business is the relationship of trust that he holds with his clients. By constantly updating his knowledge and his network he stays ahead of his clients' needs, keeping them aware of what they need to do to adapt to the new world.

BUILDING A VIRTUAL BUSINESS

William explained that his is a new model for doing business and that it has five areas of focus. These are divided into whether he is looking for width or depth in his network.

Network width provides William with:

- Access to the knowledge and connections across many platforms and into the minds of many people
- Branding tools within social media that enable him to create a wide following and a known, trusted brand
- The ability to be seen and heard by many.

Network depth enables William to:

- Test the integrity and ability of potential partners and suppliers. Through face-to-face meetings and conversations William can isolate the people he wants to partner with
- Constantly resourcing new skills and finding new partners to broaden his appeal enables him to widen his business offerings and stay ahead of his clients in terms of being able to always fulfil the needs they will have in the future.

USING DEPTH TO BUILD YOUR BUSINESS

Let's review what we have discovered in this chapter. We have focused our thoughts on building deeper meaning and depth within our networks. Abha was a prime example of someone who focused on community first and as a result has created her business from all the things she has learned about her value to others and her awareness of the needs of others.

She achieved this through building friendships and through conversations.

We also saw how Dave Clarke has created advocates for his business through his networking at face-to-face events and within a niche private group called BlackStar. Within this group he found people who wanted to tell others about his lunchtime network and also become business partners.

Finally, we have just examined the business model and process that William Buist applies to developing a deep network that enables him to offer an extended level of expertise to his clients, while keeping his business costs low and adaptable.

I now want to look at another aspect of creating depth in your network through two case studies. The first is of a woman using FriendFeed to build her knowledge around her expertise, the second of a man using Socialmedian to learn a whole new subject and become an expert in it. Through these two sites these people have created a niche network around them that serves their need for staying ahead of the game, and in doing this they are creating new opportunities for their future.

FEEDING YOURSELF WITH KNOWLEDGE

I have stated several times that knowledge is the main component that will allow you to leverage social media and build attraction. It is the food that nourishes you. Sharing your knowledge will create a network around you that will advocate or buy from you.

Sally Church, based in New Jersey, USA, is focused on the pharmaceutical industry.[58] She runs a boutique marketing strategy company and in addition to her website – http://www.icarusconsultants.com – Sally writes a regular blog

– www.pharmastrategyblog.com. She is very active across many social media platforms, running groups and helping others. I have been aware of Sally for more than four years. I looked back at the messages between Sally and me and saw we first exchanged one in April 2005, a long time in the internet world! One of Sally's messages said, 'Two lovely ladies wrote to me within minutes of each other about nutrition and cancer, so it seemed sensible to connect them together and now they are both thrilled to be sharing their passion with each other, which makes me very happy.' You get a sense from this that Sally is a giver and loves to help people. Sally has become increasingly brilliant at leveraging the internet and has many followers and fans.

While I was researching information for my book I did a search about FriendFeed to see who had knowledge as a user. I came across a comment that Sally added to a blog on Ecademy about FriendFeed and sent her a message to ask her for her experience of this site. As a result of this random search Sally and I were once again connected, and I want to pass on her knowledge of FriendFeed to you and help you to see how she has utilized it. This will give you some ideas of how FriendFeed can help you to create depth and increase your knowledge in your chosen field of expertise.

Sally's business is focused on large corporates in the pharmaceutical and biotechnology industries. Sally is a very bright lady and her qualifications are impressive. She received a B.Sc. (Hons) in Sports Science, M.Sc. in Human & Applied Physiology and Ph.D. in Respiratory Medicine from the University of London (King's College Hospital). She has attended executive education in finance at Harvard Business School and gained an executive MBA from Rutgers. We are dealing here with a lady who has a brain and a big heart, the perfect combination.

I was fascinated that Sally advised me that FriendFeed allows her to follow and interact with people brighter and smarter than her, which must take some doing! What she loves is that when new sites emerge it appears to be the brightest and smartest that engage inside them, an interesting observation that has been confirmed to me a number of times. Many people think it is people with time on their hands that spend time on the internet. Over and over again this theory is proven wrong: the internet actually gives people more time. Bright people know that.

Sally was encouraged to join FriendFeed by reading recommendations from people she admired on the internet, including Louis Gray (you read about his blogging on page 144). She was told that FriendFeed was a place to have more meaningful conversations with like-minded people. Sally soon found that inside FriendFeed there were many conversations about science, technology and life in general. She joined a utility they launched called 'Rooms', finding her perfect 'room' to be the 'Life Scientist Room'. This group started out very niche, with conversations around complex scientific data, but in time it grew and at the point of my chat with Sally there were 666 people in the 'room'.

Inside the 'Life Scientist Room' Sally interacts with fellow scientists, many in the field of cancer, her specialization. She has met up with some of these people at cancer conferences. All of the people in her FriendFeed network share their blogs and comment on them in FriendFeed. Sally feeds her blog into the site and has many followers. As a result of this close networking, Sally feels her science blogging is improving as it is read by people she admires and that she can learn from.

Sally summed up her experience saying that online it is about having the heart and passion to find people with similar interests. For Sally these interests are pharmaceutical, science, technology, social media and marketing. Thanks to Twitter and FriendFeed she can bring these subjects together and build her knowledge and her network.

What is interesting about Sally is her thirst for knowledge and it is clear that this is one of her skills. Gathering the knowledge and sharing it with others is creating a trusted network around her that advocates and likes her. While Sally's network may be growing, it has depth and has tremendous value for her personally and in her business life.

Finally, I asked Sally what the centre of her social media strategy was. In other words, from which place on the internet did she leverage her brand and build her network? The answer is her blog. Once again, the aspect of being known and sharing knowledge is confirmed as the critical starting point for a skilled social media user. Once her blog is written and updated several times a week, Sally then feeds it into Twitter, FriendFeed, Facebook and Ecademy. These feeds are critical for building awareness and visibility and sharing her thoughts with her followers.

STARTING OUT – AN ENTREPRENEUR'S JOURNEY INTO SOCIAL MEDIA

One thing that is guaranteed when you begin your journey on the internet is that it will seem a muddle. There is a long way to go before structure and clarity are built into the internet, in fact, the lack of structure is part of the change that we have to embrace. I think this 'muddle' is creating a calming influence: where there is mystery there is sharing and collaboration; where there are people helping one another to learn, there is progress. These are the inherent values that I love about the internet.

I admire all the early adopters and the people who are creating the change, and I admire the open-minded, trusting way in which many entrepreneurs are spending their time inside social media. One such entrepreneur is Nick Tadd.[59] I interviewed Nick for my book as he is a progressive, determined man, with a great big heart who is spending his time working out how he can leverage the internet to make him money. I met Nick on Ecademy and his journey and his thoughts will mirror that of anyone who is starting out and seeing what social media is all about.

Nick is a property man, with past experience of the TV and music industry. He has made his living from speaking as a property expert and from having a number of properties that he rents. Nick also has a portfolio of customers for whom he manages their property interests. Nick has developed his property business and network with his wife Vanessa within social media since 2006 and has a successful website – www.4wallsandaceiling.com.

Nick is like many people in business, as he is busy and focused on his current business but thankfully he has also invested a great deal of time learning social media. Recently, like many millions of people, Nick has seen a change in his business due to the economic environment. In Nick's words, 'My clients are not the people with the money any more.' Many of his clients are suffering due to property prices falling and the lack of investment in property. Nick has realized that his involvement with social media, which was at first a marketing avenue for his core business, is now going to be his future. This is one very big lesson for anyone embarking into the world of social media. It is not just a new marketing channel, it is an industry in its own right and the future of social media is strong. Learning how you can adapt your current business model to be part of social media rather than on the outside of it will ensure your survival.

I discussed this in Chapter five, *Looking back to look forwards* – highlighting that some businesses saw e-commerce purely as a sales channel whereas others saw it as a whole new way of doing business. It was the entrepreneurs who saw the opportunity of e-commerce as a different way of doing business that have survived and become the success stories. Nick will be one of the survivors because he is going to do things differently.

Doing things differently depends on what you do. The basic premise for everyone is to look at your business and decide whether you are able to learn fast and adapt to this different opportunity. Nick was very open and shared a great deal in his conversation with me. He said he didn't have all the answers yet, but in his words, 'No one knows where the money is, but if you're not even on the playing field you have no chance of scoring the goal.' This is one of the most important lessons I can teach you. Social media is still a muddle and you have to learn to cope with that. In fact, it is the people like Nick who accept this and go with the flow that will be the ones to make the money. It is the ultimate leap of faith. You just have to start learning how to play the game and be part of the movement as the rules are created.

Nick has kept his ear firmly to the ground through social media sites. Here are his top five:

1. **Ecademy** serves him as his community, his test pad for ideas, his apprenticeship in social media and the place where he can be himself and learn alongside like-minded, supportive people. Nick has created a private club on Ecademy for his thoughts and his creation of his blogs. Ecademy is so rich in what it gives business owners in terms of tools for search engine optimization, HTML code

and groups, and Nick utilizes these tools to create his content for use on all the other social media sites.

2. **Socialmedian** provides him with real-time news clippings about anything to do with social media, meaning he is learning all the time from the 'gurus' of the industry.

3. **Twitter** has become a place where he broadcasts what he learns and through this he has accumulated 5,400 followers who relate him to social media. This positions him inside this world rather than on the outside looking in.

4. **Ning** has enabled him to build his own social network around property. This is a very recent addition to his strategy and here he will teach other property people how to leverage social media.

5. **Google Reader** provides him with information according to the feeds he has set up.

Through embedding himself inside the social media community he has learned how to be part of it, not just be a user of the tools. In Nick's words, 'The future is going to happen, so I need to be part of it.' I have seen many people treat social media purely as a channel for referrals or sales leads. They are staying deeply rooted in the old world, they are not adapting to the fact that social media is actually a new business model and will become the dominant way that people in the future communicate, collaborate and build their businesses.

As a result of Nick's desire to learn about social media for his property business he has built a network of experts around him. He is utilizing Socialmedian to find the knowledge he wants and is sending links all over the internet into sites to alert others about what he is reading and learning; Twitter is his main 'engine' for this. Nick has now become part of the social media world. He is now associated with the best people and his brand is becoming associated with social media as well as property. This puts him well ahead of others and enables him to build a new business model for the new world.

Nick's followers on Twitter have more conversations with him about social media than they do about property. As a result of his pioneering spirit Nick is now working on several business ideas that he knows will take him out of the old world and into the new world of commerce. Nick is naturally a conversationalist, preferring depth to width; however, he has learnt that the wider his network has become the more conversations he has had. Having conversations with strangers is advancing his knowledge and understanding of what people are looking for and where the opportunities lie.

Nick's final words were, 'Every bone in my body tells me this is the right thing to do but I am still making sense of it and learning how to leverage it.' I asked him, if he won the lottery what would he do? His reply was, 'I would still remain on Ecademy as that is where my friends are.' It is not just about the money to Nick, it is the people that matter.

BUILD YOUR BUSINESS FROM THE INSIDE OUT

When we looked at 'know me', we saw that network width enables your business to be known while depth builds your business. The case studies I have shared in this chapter all show how people are using the same tools as those who are using them to be 'known', but are using them differently. Each of the people highlighted here has turned to the community to learn and make their business stronger. They have built their businesses differently and they have created new opportunities for themselves.

'Like me' is about conversations, getting to know people

and learning new things. However good you think you are, there are even better minds around the world and they really want to connect with you, your mind and your contacts. No man is an island; humans do not thrive when they isolate themselves from others. There has been a temptation to be independent, proud and stand tall among the other tall trees, but you don't have to any more. There are people out there who want to be your friend and who want you to thrive. This is the philosophy I talked about at the beginning of my book. The people who shared their stories in this chapter validated this fact. People are caring more and you can be part of that new world if you take the time to talk. Connecting minds is the future, and perhaps connecting hearts is the method for doing this. Inside communities, you connect hearts.

CHAPTER 9

FOLLOW ME – CREATING SOCIAL TRANSACTIONS

THE THIRD AND final part of the 'know me, like me, follow me' process is turning your followers into friends who you care about and who understand you and your needs. Once you have people who are following you closely you will have a concentrated group that know what knowledge you hold and what values you share. These people are your ultimate advocates and the most valuable part of your network. These people are your 'business friends'.

Ultimately, when you achieve the status of 'follow me' you are creating significant influence within social media. Having followers and friends requires people to know you, like you and respect you. Creating deep friendships requires you to know your place within the social media world and to know exactly what to contribute. By the stage of creating followers and friends you will have clarity about your expertise, you will be sharing knowledge and you will be liked. The volume of followers and business friends you have will depend on how wide and deep your network is. This is when you will see the benefit of building network that encompasses both.

US

'Follow me' is very much about 'us', the collective 'us'. It is about being involved in something greater than just you, yet it is the most attractive part of being you as it reflects all that you want to contribute and share for the greater good of others. Your ability to be followed will depend on your ability to be a 'leader'. Not a leader in the traditional sense, this is not about leading a team, but leading a movement and a set of thoughts.

Look back to Chapter three (see page 45) and recall the story of Hannah and the way she shared her revision notes with her friends. This is the 'us' in the philosophy of the new world, unconditional giving and thinking about the whole, not the individual gain.

There is confusion surrounding followers. What makes someone a follower? Can you say that all people that follow you, know and like you? Not in all cases. You may have more than 1,000 followers on Twitter, but have they just clicked a button and said 'follow' or do they actually know you, trust you and like you?

To me, a 'follower' is someone who has decided that they want to engage with you regularly, receive updates to your blogs and learn from you. Your followers want to access your mind and your inner thoughts. This is like having 'fans' in the celebrity world. You may have a very wide network, lots of people may like you, but the real value in your network is those people that have decided that you are the ultimate expert in your field of knowledge. They trust you to provide the contacts and people that will help them to keep up to date on anything that is in your sphere of knowledge.

The process of 'know me, like me, follow me' indicates that the number of people in each section reduces, but your relationships become more intense. Thomas believes that one in one hundred of your 'know me' network may 'like you'. One in a thousand will become a follower.

Consider this network:

- 10,000 'know me' – my network size on Twitter, LinkedIn, Ecademy, YouTube etc.
- 100 'like me' – those I have a dialogue with, may have met, they talk about me
- 10 'follow me' – those that I have a shared meaning with and can collaborate with and help – my friends.

This is why it is critical to create a wide network and then create depth within it. You cannot create the golden nugget of having followers unless you have put in the time and the skills that create this level of trust and appreciation.

I am being very strict about this as I know that many people are blindly building networks, having lots of conversations, but unless they have a goal in mind and create a brand that creates this level of depth there is a danger that they are only creating noise. I want you to build a brand that makes you money and creates a sustainable, adaptable business to create personal wealth for you and your followers. That is the icing on the cake – when your time, energy and knowledge also help others to make money, that is 'winning by sharing', a wonderful phrase created by Leon Benjamin, Ecademy shareholder and consultant.[60] That is the opportunity that this new connected world delivers.

Later I am going to share case studies on two people who have created groups inside Ecademy and how that is helping them build their following and build their brand. At the same time they have created an ecosystem within which others can learn, develop and become wealthier, a shared place, where no one person gains at the expense of another.

To create a following takes a new type of leadership, without tasks, without control and without secrecy. It takes a person who knows that people want open, random and supportive leadership, people need to trust the intentions of the leader and trust that the desired outcome will be created together.

TWENTY-FIRST-CENTURY LEADERSHIP

The amount of information being delivered in books and courses into companies about the way people should lead now is enormous. 'Servant leadership' is a popular theory. It encourages leaders to serve others while staying focused on achieving results in line with the organization's values and integrity. My observation on leading a community of people is that you cannot force people to follow you, you cannot 'recruit' people into your team. Leadership has to be earned, you are placed in this role by those who follow you, not because you say 'I am a leader'.

I found this excellent quote on Wikipedia when I was looking for thoughts on servant leadership.[61] In approximately 600 BC, the Chinese sage Lao Tzu wrote the *Tao Te Ching*:

The greatest leader forgets himself
And attends to the development of others.
Good leaders support excellent workers.
Great leaders support the bottom ten percent.
Great leaders know that
The diamond in the rough
Is always found 'in the rough'.

What I love about this idea is that 'the diamonds are in the rough', yet so many of us are fearful of networking with random, unknown, untargeted people. Your diamond, your follower, will be in the rough right now. It also states that great leaders forget themselves. Many people have created groups on the internet and thought that this was their leadership tool to 'tell', to 'control' and to 'dominate'. The reality is that those people have not succeeded. Their groups have remained empty of content and empty of people and once followed, they soon become 'unfollowed'.

This is the hardest transition for anyone that is from a corporate background or currently working in a corporate business. The old world of leadership was created by job titles, organization charts, objectives, delegation, control and, dare I say, fear. Autocratic behaviour was commonplace. Although I know this is changing in many companies, this is the toughest of transitions and one that in many cases is being led by the 'workers', not by the leaders. In the twenty-first century people are rebelling against control and often see the behaviour of these types of 'leaders' as bullying and as a result feel intimidated. Under this type of leadership ideas and innovation are rare. Fear of ridicule and the time spent following objectives and tasks stops creativity and this reduces innovation and the ability to adapt.

In this section I will look at Twitter, the most recent social media tool, which has created such a noise around the thought of having followers. FriendFeed, where people may subscribe to your content, and having people subscribe to your blogs through RSS (Really Simple Syndication) feeds are other ways in which you can create a following. Remember these are the tools – they are the technology that enables you to connect and share, but just using them will not mean you have followers. At all times you have to remember the philosophy that I talked about throughout the first half of the book. There are no shortcuts. To have followers you need to have the right intention and care deeply about the success of others. Social media is the most transparent form of media and if you are trying to lead within it without contributing or caring you will never succeed. Social media has a lasting memory. What others say about you will be found forever.

'Know me, like me, follow me' is a process. Having followers is the pot of gold at the end of the rainbow. It provides you with permission to talk and share the information that matters to you and it will be read by people that you want to influence and that will advocate you. If you ever try to sell to them your journey with them will be over. Having followers may create an environment where people may like to buy from you, but that should never be why you are leading. Leading with this hidden agenda will be picked up on so fast that you will not stand a chance.

Think back to Louis Gray, the master blogger I interviewed in Chapter seven (see page 144). Louis started off writing about Silicon Valley, technology and social media because it was a hobby and an interest. In time, he had some people attempt to offer him money to write about their start-up, but he refused it. Louis is contributing and winning without putting money at the top of his agenda. That is why he is trusted and that is why so many subscribe to his blog. Louis has become a leader in social media, a man people trust and follow and while his 'know me' network reaches into many tens of thousands, his 'follow me' network is also growing because he is taking time to ensure others grow and learn with him in real time. Louis does not see anyone as his competitor, that world no longer exists.

Why do people follow and create leaders?

- Because they trust them
- Because they like them
- Because they feel supported
- Because they like their thoughts
- Because they understand their intention.

You will create a following once you can tick these boxes:

☐ I know my intention, wider than just the chance of making an income
☐ I know what knowledge I want to share
☐ I know who I can support best
☐ I want to help others be successful
☐ I will not dominate my followers
☐ I will share and be open with everything I learn.

INFLUENCE

There is a power you can achieve inside social media and that is one of influence. This is when you have enough of a following and have created enough trust and likeability that your presence influences others. The wonderful aspect of the internet is that this 'power' is bestowed on you, it cannot be bought and it cannot be created through bullying. Imagine a world where that power existed outside of the internet.

Actually we don't need to imagine it. The story of Barack Obama is the most incredible example of how a social media campaign created global followers and resulted in a relatively unknown man becoming president of the United States.

In 2007, Obama hired twenty-four-year-old Chris Hughes to run his social media campaign. Chris was one of the four founders of Facebook and left Facebook to help Obama become president. This turned out to be a key component in the success of Obama's campaign.

Chris created a new website called My.BarackObama.com. Affectionately named MyBo, this was the place on the internet that you landed on if you went to his main website – www.barackobama.com – and clicked on the link. MyBo immediately made you feel that his campaign was about 'you' and enabled you to become part of his community. From the point of joining you were presented with a place to have a voice and a way of sharing what mattered to you. You could watch videos, go to events, create events, share photos and write your own blog. Critically you could follow Obama in whatever social network you wanted to.

Just look at the difference between Obama and McCain the day before he won the election, 3 November 2007.

	Obama	McCain	Percentage of followers Obama had over McCain
Facebook supporters	2,379,102	620,359	383%
MySpace friends	833,161	217,811	382%
YouTube subscribers	114,559	28,419	403%
YouTube channel views	18,413,110	2,0232,993	910%
Twitter	112,474	4,603	2443%

Statistics provided by Jeremiah Owyang www.web-strategist.com/blog

Obama and Chris Hughes saw the opportunity of social media and they worked it. Obama put up 1,792 videos into his YouTube channel while McCain only had 329. Obama has continued to engage within social media. As of spring 2009, four months after his election, he has more than half a million followers in Twitter and provides them with updates encouraging continual involvement in their America.

Barack Obama has built a following because people feel they can trust him. He uses emotional words and he shares his thoughts openly. He has talked about one world and he gives the impression that he seeks peace. Obama is completely in line with the desires of a large number of people and he resonates the change that many want to see in the world. People could feel the drumbeat he created across all media, people 'liked him' and people 'followed him'. His social media website enabled people to create community groups and 'get involved', his followers became his personal army. It is those followers that ensured he became president of the United States of America, getting his message out on to the streets. With a huge network, he created a 'like me' status and the followers turned up, became volunteers for his campaign and knew exactly what they needed to do to win the election through social networks, video, events and Twitter. It is the most phenomenal advocacy campaign we have ever witnessed.

Barack Obama displays all the qualities of being open, random and supportive; the closed, selective and controlling attitudes reside in past leaders.

MEASURING YOUR NETWORK

In an ideal world we would love to run our networks like we ran our CRM (customer relationship management) systems. When I started in business we had a box of index cards on every salesperson's desk, and it was divided into three:

- **Market** – those people who we knew existed but did not

have a relationship with our company – our suspects
- **Working** – those people who we were talking to but had yet to get them to buy from us – our prospects
- **Buying** – our customers

This is over twenty-five years ago, and the system was very simplistic. Of course, we soon brought in computers and spent thousands on a CRM system with which we could analyze ourselves to our hearts' desire. This kept many managers in a job. I fear that at times I became this type of manager. I am not saying business does not need analysis and lots of reflection and planning. Board meetings are rituals about numbers and governance and analysis is necessary. My point here is that marketing cannot be treated as a numbers game in the same way as we used to. Finding opportunities and evolving a business is about absorbing information and connecting with people at hyperspeed. Learning to filter is the art now, not blocking out thoughts and people to ensure our lives are controllable and predictable.

The need to understand our market still remains strong in us all. The world of buying a list of targets and working through them with a marketing campaign to get them to eventually buy was targeted, systematic and measurable. It suited the corporate world as you could measure input and train people to be better at opening and closing a deal. If their results were good you could give them a bonus or a pay rise, if they were bad you could fire them! How neat and tidy that was – structured, controllable and hierarchical.

Now, the world is different. Your brand is being created by anyone who wants to talk about it, your opportunities come from left field, not from where you targeted, and your staff do not want to be controlled, measured and managed, they want to be trusted and supported. They want to believe in you and your intention, they want to share the goals of the business and know that there are no secrets. They no longer want to live in fear.

Applying my original teachings of market, working, buying, I created 'know me, like me, follow me'. The latter is the networked equivalent of the former.

- Market – 'Know me' – your strangers (used to be called Suspects)
- Working – 'Like me' – your friends (used to be called Prospects)
- Buying – 'Follow me' – your advocates and your followers (used to be called Customers)

MEASURING 'KNOW ME'

It is possible to add up all the people in your networks and have a guide as to how many people 'know you'. The fact that they are in your network assumes that at some time they clicked on your profile and they agreed to communicate with you, but most remain a 'stranger to you'. Of course, your brand may be bigger than that, and the more you can invite people into your network using 'invitation' tools (which all reputable networks have), the more you can get your arms around the people that know you and be able to communicate with them regularly. Think back to how Hannah is not fearful of embracing new people into her network because she knows that the combination of the technology will enable her to do this very easily. I collect business cards from everyone I meet and use the Ecademy invitation tool to invite them into my network of friends. Instantly I can stay in touch forever.

MEASURING 'LIKE ME'

This is very subjective. On Ecademy we enable people to tag people as their 'spotlight', the people they like. For me those are the people on Ecademy that I want to communicate with regularly. This is an area that many of the networks could become better at, allowing you to segment people into those that you are building a relationship with, over time. Certainly on Ecademy we will increasingly develop code for this. Conversation is critical and it is impossible to have a conversation with everyone, but you need to keep in touch with those that you do have this dialogue with.

The great aspect of being able to tag people as 'like' or move into a place where you know you can communicate regularly in a community is that you can also see who has chosen to put you in their 'spotlight' (an Ecademy term), which is a measurement of who likes you. This allows you to measure the opinions of others regarding your contribution.

MEASURING 'FOLLOW ME'

When I talk about this form of 'follow me' I am not talking about how many follow you on Twitter. Your followers on Twitter are your wide, 'know me' part of your strategy. As I said earlier, Thomas is of the opinion, drawn from years of analysis and research, that only one in a thousand people in your wide, 'know me' network will actually want to follow you. This is the case if you are building a wide network, and we believe you should. However, some may have a smaller, more intimate network and they may create a higher ratio of followers than that, but you need to keep feeding your network with people at the top to stop your network and your knowledge becoming stale.

Measuring people who want to be close to you and actually follow you can be done in several ways. It is a measurement of the influence you are having through your social media interaction.

I am fearful that you can become too caught up in this analysis, so please be mindful of the fact that this is only measuring traffic and, to a certain extent, your ability to draw people to you. This is very objective. What matters most is what people say about you and whether they like and trust you. This goes back to making sure that you don't treat social media purely as a tool; there are people behind everything you see and do, always remember that. Nothing replaces conversation so, when you can, arrange face-to-face meetings to really build a following.

RSS FEEDS

RSS is the format on the web for distributing news and other web content. RSS feeds keep your audience constantly updated and allow people to see your content without having to go to your website or blog. This increases the chances of having followers as it reduces the risk of someone visiting your site, liking what they read and then forgetting to visit again! I see this as the next stage on from e-mailed newsletters but it relies on you creating content that is compelling and helps people move forward in their own knowledge or thinking.

When we looked at creating a 'know me' presence, we looked in depth at blogging, examining the way that Louis Gray has created a following around his observations of social media (see page 144). We know that Louis has over 65,000 people visiting his blog each month. Louis is most interested in the 4,700 that subscribe to his RSS feed. This means that they have requested that they are 'fed' his blogs as he writes them. This is a true measure of a follower as this person wants to ensure that they always read Louis' thoughts. Louis has a very wide network across many social media platforms. Ultimately he measures his followers as those who subscribe to him in FriendFeed and those that subscribe to his blog.

The detail of how to create RSS feeds from your site and 'feed' people with your content is readily available on the internet through searches on Google. I am not creating a 'how to' guide here, I want you to purely understand the context. The starting point is being a creator of content. This is the only way that others can follow you and, more critically, advocate your content.

Louis also utilizes FriendFeed as a resource to enable him to create a following around all his content – from his blog and from other places as well – helping to put all of his diverse activity in one place and presenting a platform for discussion so his followers can know him better. You know from earlier mentions of FriendFeed that this site allows you to create a distinct group around the subjects that really matter to you rather than a broad network. Inside FriendFeed, Louis can distribute his knowledge to people that he knows are following his knowledge. Louis is in the top twenty most followed people in Friendfeed (in early April 2009 he was at number 16). Louis has over 7,000 followers. These are true followers, drilled down from a very large 'know me' network.

TWITTER

Twitter has to be mentioned in this chapter as it epitomizes 'follow me', yet I am cautious about this. Twitter is about creating a wide network and sits best in 'know me'. However, there are some very clever utilities that serve Twitter that will help you to see how much you are being talked about and how much influence you have.

The following tools are ways that Thomas measures his influence and his following.

TWITTER COUNTER
http://www.twittercounter.com

Twitter Counter shows Thomas how he is progressing inside Twitter. If your network slows up you know that your content is deteriorating or that you are not active across enough networks. People see Thomas contributing inside Ecademy, Facebook, LinkedIn and FriendFeed, and because he was able to secure 'thomaspower' (all one word) on Twitter, he is easily searched and followed. Twitter Counter also shows you how you are growing by day and your rank in the world and by country. These are important measurements if you want to be one of the top connectors and social media people in your geographical area. This can matter. Increasingly people are looking at these sites to find people who can help them as they trade in an ever increasing number of countries to become global. Note that Twitter Counter only tells you what rank you are in a country; to know who the top twitterer in each country and city is use Twitter Grader.

Twitter Counter also allows you to embed a counter into

your social network profiles, blogs or website to show how many followers you have, once again displaying your network size.

TWITTER ANALYZER
http://www.twitteranalyzer.com

Twitter Analyzer does what is says – it analyzes your Twitter activity. This is a list of some of the things you can look at:

• How many readers have been exposed to your messages?
• Who re-tweets your messages?
• Twitter follower stats?
• Twitter followers' growth rate?
• What are other people writing about you?
• How popular are you?

Thomas is most interested in who is following him so he can choose the information that they would most like to read.

He knows who his most 'loyal' followers are and also he knows what profession they are in. All of the above analysis provides a way to see your growth. Analyzing is something we can get hung up on, but kept in context it is useful. I would suggest that tracking your Twitter audience will give you an understanding of the vibration you are sending out and if you are not getting the results in your business that you hope for, perhaps this will give you some clues as to why.

TWINFLUENCE
http://www.twinfluence.com/

This is a very fast way of seeing the number of people that are following you and how many people are following them. This indicates the opportunity for your content to be 're-tweeted', creating a way to reach out further.

By very quickly adding your Twitter name and password you will be advised how many friends/followers you have and what your 'second-order' follower number is. So at the point of writing this book Thomas had 7,016 followers and his second-order followers were 16.4 million – a great reach when looking for people and knowledge and equally when sharing information with others. There are no surprises that Thomas is 're-tweeted' a great deal as he acts as a middleman and provides knowledge and contacts at a tremendous rate.

CREATING FOLLOWERS ON TWITTER

At an event that I chaired recently, I was impressed by a gentleman called Dirk Singer.[62] He spoke about social media and his clarity around Twitter encouraged me to interview him as a case study. What struck me when we talked was Dirk's philosophy, which was 'I am followed on Twitter because I share.'

Dirk is a founding partner at Cow – www.thisiscow.com – a brand communication and PR company. Dirk runs two blogs and is very active on Twitter. He loves social media and advises FMCG (fast-moving consumer goods) clients on how to create, embrace and take the leap into the new world of social media. Dirk is an analyst, a strategist, a planner and loves to report on trends.

On Twitter, Dirk is known as 'dirkthecow' and has (at the time of writing) 2,116 followers and has posted 2,973 updates.

Dirk says that the two sites he uses the most are delicious – www.delicious.com – for bookmarking content and Twitter for sharing information. The information he shares is about marketing, business trends and social media and his followers know him for this. For Dirk, the number of followers on Twitter indicates his network size, but what matters to him is how many people subscribe to his blog. This indicates that measuring the number of people that he can 'feed' his blog to provide him with a real sense of who follow him.

Dirk also uses Tweetdeck – www.tweetdeck.com – a very important utility to enable you to sort the noise. Tweetdeck will increasingly help you sort out the noise of all your social media activity. For now, it is most associated with Twitter and enables users to split their main Twitter feed, which is all your followers, into columns. This is a critical application when you become a Twitter user as it allows you to organize your inform-ation on Twitter into people that you want to keep close, your favourites and the public and direct messages that you are receiving. Dirk is interested in those people that have chosen him as one of their favourites. This is the true mark of a follower, rather than just someone that you have in your wide network.

Tweetdeck sits as a tool on your toolbar and can constantly alert you to new information that is landing in your deck. I believe that in the future there will be a 'war' between these viewing and organizing utilities in the same way that we saw the browser wars in the 1990s. Already www.seesmic.com is emerging as a strong contender. The way you view your Twitter updates is very important and there is still some way to go before they are presenting the information the way we all want it.

'Re-tweeting' is also a way of seeing how many times

Dirk's content is shared – Twitter Analyzer can supply this information. Dirk also likes the new facility of hashtags. One of these is '#followfriday' (or now known as #ff) – this is a great way of people advocating others on a Friday. How often you are mentioned as someone to follow is a great indication of the respect and likeability you have created inside the community.

For anyone wanting to see when they are being talked about, Twitter Search is great. Placing your name or brand into the search area of Twitter will bring up a list of all the recent 'tweets' that you have been referred to; this is worth watching occasionally.

Hashtags are becoming very important for searching. Hashtags were developed as a means to create a 'grouping' effect on Twitter, without having to change the basic service. Adding a '#' to your brand or subject in your tweet will enable people to search on that information. I add '#ecademy' to my entries when they are about Ecademy members or content. This way I can look at the search in Twitter and get a sense of the conversations that are taking place around Ecademy. Many people do this. Hashtagging can allow you to set up an instant group for a short time, for example around an event you are running. By advising your network that the event will have this '#' tag in your tweets and requesting that they also add it creates a lot of noise around instant news items or events. I talked earlier about Thomas setting up Twalkes. They created #Twalk on the day of their first walk, and #Twalk became a top ten trending topic for two hours on Twitter.

The critical learning point from Dirk is that you have to create value through sharing information and not be seduced into thinking that because you have a large network you have followers. Dirk knows how to see his true followers and he knows that the value he holds in those people reflects the contribution he is making to them through his knowledge.

I SHARE CONTENT THAT IS USEFUL, WHAT DO YOU DO?

There is one final point that I want to make on the sharing of content. 'I share content that is useful, what do you do?' Aron Stevenson had entered a comment on a blog and I saw this phrase tagged in his signature.[63] I just loved it. It totally sums up the world we live in now. 'I share content that is useful' could perhaps be the most critical thing you could learn about social media. I have now connected with Aron and have advocated him many times on Twitter and in Ecademy, just like that! I believe Aron is one of the few that really 'get it'.

MEASUREMENT – KEEPING IT IN PERSPECTIVE

I want to finish this section with a warning: this is an open, unstructured, fast-moving, random world. You must keep the measurement of your influence, traffic and following in perspective. Use it as a way of seeing whether you are developing your visibility, but at all times remember that it is what people are saying about you that matters, not just how often you are being talked about! In Ivan Misner's great words 'you need visibility and credibility to achieve profitable relationships'.

BUILDING YOUR OWN COMMUNITY – YOUR MICRO-SOCIAL NETWORK

The subject of the final part of this chapter is possibly your ultimate goal – creating your own community of followers. If you can say 'yes' to the following then perhaps you are ready to start your own group and lead others into success.

- I have such a strong sense of what I want to contribute.
- I have a deep understanding of my expertise.
- I have a depth of knowledge that I want to share openly.
- My network is growing with people that know me, like me, trust me and want to follow me.
- I believe in new leadership with open, random and supportive thoughts.
- I know the overall intention that we can all share in.

When you have all of these ticked you may be ready to build your own social community and run a group.

Many people create groups online and inside communities such as Facebook, LinkedIn, Ecademy and Ning. This enables a level of independence and branding, but success is hard to achieve without all the qualities I listed above. Critically, you must be a twenty-first-century leader and know how to lead with all the values and philosophies that we have talked about throughout this book.

HOW TO LEVERAGE YOUR NETWORK AND CREATE THE ULTIMATE 'FOLLOW ME' NETWORK

I would like to share a case study with you of a great guy called Philip Calvert, who has successfully created a group around his experience of financial services and is now making a living from his own community and contribution inside social media.[64] I have chosen Philip as he has made the transition through every aspect that I have talked about: he has a philosophy of sharing and contributing, he has a great online network, he spends time getting to know people and he has been very clear about the knowledge he shares and how he can help others.

In 2004 after twenty-five years in financial services corporate life, Philip was made redundant. He was given a good farewell cheque, which gave him time to review life and realize that commuting and 'pointless' meetings were not what he wanted to have in his life any more. During a meeting at the Professional Speakers Association, Philip heard about Ecademy as a community of people who had also moved from corporate life into being self-employed. He joined and discovered that he had a great deal in common with other members.

Being part of a community of other self-employed people, Philip decided to set up a marketing consulting company helping independent financial advisers (IFAs) and financial planners. Philip started a group on Ecademy for IFAs and although Ecademy didn't have many IFAs in its membership at the time, Philip spread the word at industry conferences and events and encouraged them to join his group on Ecademy.

The intention of the IFA group, called IFA Life, was to enable IFAs to network online, share best practice, debate industry issues and receive marketing tips from Philip. Being on Ecademy also gave the IFAs that joined a marketplace to promote themselves to people who needed pensions, mortgages and investment advice.

By 2008 IFA Life had reached 500 members inside Ecademy. Philip sent out regular press releases to industry press and wrote articles about how IFAs need to learn to network online. Philip was attracting people from outside of Ecademy to join his group. By using the invitation tools on Ecademy to send invites this ensured that when they joined Ecademy they automatically became a member of IFA Life.

Philip could then continue a dialogue with them and immediately give them value with the content and people inside the group.

Philip has a great analogy for how to keep conversation going inside a group online. 'I ran the group as though it was a fish tank, the members were the fish. Every day I sprinkled food into the tank in the shape of quick tips, links, ideas, resources and articles.' This goes back to the importance of sharing knowledge and having the members' needs and success at the forefront of your mind. Philip's goal was always to add value to their lives and he noticed that providing he kept adding food, the fish would consume it. Philip did this every day for four years. As time went on he noticed that if he missed a day, the fish still came to look for it and in time they started creating the food together, relying less and less on Philip to be their keeper. They began to contribute their own thoughts, ideas and comments.

The benefit that Philip saw in time was that his consulting grew. The trust he was building within the IFA community enabled him to get more clients. He also ran events that he charged a fee to attend. This further added to his opportunity to give value to the members and in return the value that he was getting from it also grew.

In January 2008 one of his members suggested to him that it may be time for him to go out on his own. The press was talking about niche social networking sites and with a great brand, a good network and the knowledge of leading a group on Ecademy, Philip felt ready to set up a networking site of his own. He invested his own money, found suppliers within his network on Ecademy and created www.ifalife.com, a social network for financial advisers.

By February 2009 they were on target for 2,000 members and had a plan in place for a further 3,000 to join. Philip spends almost nothing on marketing his site, he uses social media and feeds content via RSS feed to Twitter, LinkedIn, Socialmedian and Digg. Through this he attracts new members to his network. By using Google Alerts, Twitter and LinkedIn Answers he adds his comments and advice whenever financial services are being talked about.

Philip still leads the IFA group on Ecademy in parallel to his own social network. He feeds the network and encourages the use of both. Through this he is adding value and also optimizing his groups on Google.

Traditional marketing remains important to Philip through articles, press releases and offline events – with some attracting sponsorship. Attending financial services conferences is also valuable and he often speaks at these events. When asked to pay to attend, he simply offers to promote their event on his site instead, a win-win for both parties.

Philip has created a 'know me, like me, follow me' process that works. He knows who his followers are and inside his groups he has total permission to talk about a subject he knows well. He can ensure he becomes the known expert on how businesses can increase sales through seminars and social networking websites. Philip knows how to create a lot of noise but equally how to ensure that the people hearing that noise are the right people, in his target market.

Philip has also created the gold at the end of the 'long tail'. For all his time and energy given to his network, ultimately he knows that he will achieve an income, whether through his books, his seminars or his training.

This is a great case study. The four years that Philip has spent inside social media learning, investing in and contributing to is paying off. He truly is a twenty-first-century businessman who has adapted to the new world.

UNDERSTANDING THE 'LONG TAIL' AND APPLYING IT TO SOCIAL NETWORKING GROUPS

In Chapter six I discussed the challenge and the opportunity that exist in a free economy, a market where everyone is expecting something for nothing in order to engage you and build trust. I introduced Chris Anderson who wrote the 'long tail' article in *Wired* magazine and we learned, like Philip Calvert did, that we have to find a way to contribute for free and leverage the money at the end of the 'long tail'.

Each of us has some value, knowledge and contribution that we could give away for free, we just have to create a business strategy that ensures our whole life is not entirely free for others to leverage. This can be a tough strategy to create. I want to talk now about James Knight, the creator of the IMAs, the communication profiling tool that Ecademy has adopted. We discussed this in Chapter five, *What is your natural communication style?* (see page 111).

James agreed to share his profiling tool for free on Ecademy, leveraging the network to ultimately sell seminars, e-books and events at the end of this 'long tail'. His story is inspiring and watching him utilize and embed himself inside the Ecademy community has taught me so much about creating a 'follow me' network.

Each week, 1,000 people join one of James's groups on Ecademy. They join the High Blue, High Red, High Green or High Yellow groups. As a result of this, James can now talk to an increasing 'follow me' network around the subject he is interested in and can propose events, do research and promote his knowledge, knowing that he has gained their attention and they have agreed to belong.

James wants to help people communicate more effectively and assist them in developing human relationship skills that will help them to get along with others. James has a business consulting to companies and individuals around the behavioural styles of people, regularly helping companies get more from their interaction with one another and increasing harmony and results.

We studied the four behaviour styles in Chapter five and it is clear that some are assertive, some are closed, while some people are open and non-assertive. The combination of these two aspects alone can be enough to create barriers, but James teaches other aspects of the four types and through his advice people are learning to communicate inside Ecademy with more empathy and understanding. This is a unique tool for Ecademy and for this reason we were happy to embed it inside the community as an application.

James has created a partnership with Ecademy that has ensured the visibility of his product and he has built his brand very fast from a standing start. Facebook has taken these 'partnerships with developers' a stage further and has a 'developer community', allowing them to create applications and drop them into Facebook. Social media strategists are helping many corporates engage with their audience inside social communities in this way. The corporate community are beginning to realize that engagement is more successful now than broadcast. Engagement is a long-term process, yet currently most corporates are seeing engagement as a short burst of interaction while they promote a new product. This will change.

James as a case study is cutting edge. He has learned how to create groups and has embedded his business into a community. Now he is watching his own brand grow. Interestingly, James is, to a certain extent, leapfrogging the 'know me' and 'like me' aspect of his networks. He very quickly achieves visibility and growth inside his groups, with strangers joining before he has had a chance to exchange messages or get to know them. You will read later that this was not how he started and he has created enough goodwill to manage this.

The following is an extract from the interview I had with James. You will see that James is astute and very aware of what is needed. You will also learn that James adapted his business for Ecademy members as he knew that this was a new world he was entering.

When joining Ecademy I knew that my attitude towards the people within Ecademy would determine their attitude towards me. The greatest craving of every Ecademy member is the desire to be appreciated. I knew that if I wanted Ecademy members to be interested in me that I first had to show interest in them. I wanted to be liked because people do business with people that they like.

One of the things that I looked for from Ecademy was for it to help me in my mission to produce an ever increasing number of people aware of my personality profiling system and the related products and services that I offer dealing with behaviour styles and strategies.

Ecademy has hundreds of thousands of members. One of the greatest challenges that every member faces when they begin their journey, including myself, is how to gain favourable attention and create interest in what you are doing. You need to be interesting enough so that people want to connect with you.

The most common way of gaining attention is through compliments, however this is really difficult over the internet because you run the risk of appearing insincere and putting people off you instead of making more friends and winning new business.

Another less common way of gaining attention is through a gift. I decided that I would share information with Ecademy members about something I knew they would be certain to be interested in, i.e. information about themselves and why they do what they do. Although I normally charge for consultancy and seminars I decided I would give a sampling to members as a gift to help them understand themselves and others better and to help to communicate more effectively.

James developed a questionnaire that he sent to members when they contacted him. He accompanied it with a note saying, 'To help us get acquainted would you mind answering a few questions?' As the replies came in he identified them as one of the four colours. When he wrote back to them with information regarding their behavioural traits, he would get a note back saying 'That's me!'

Enthused by this James created four images in the shape of a piece of jigsaw with a brief explanation of how people preferred to be treated. Within a few months 1,000 people had answered the questionnaire and many were displaying the puzzle on their site.

The next step for James was to create four groups on Ecademy as he knew that 'birds of a feather flock together'. If he could give people with the same traits the chance to communicate it would increase their chances of success. The concept of the groups was that 'we like people that are like us'.

It was at this stage I approached James and a meeting was arranged between him and our CEO to see how we could make the process easier for members. It was clear that this idea was popular and would enhance the opportunity for members to achieve networking success, plus it was fun.

James is now working on the marketing of events and the creation of products. He has not focused on this until he could see the value that others were gaining in the groups. He is now being asked for more information, a true reflection of his ability to lead and his desire for others to succeed. James has been given 'permission' by his followers to sell to them now. This is the ultimate result at the end of the 'long tail' and once you have created a 'know me, like me' network, the followers will come and your future will be secured.

CHAPTER 10

ARE YOU READY?

Y OU HAVE NOW read about the philosophies and the tools that will enable you to rise up as an individual and become a contributing person in your own right, to be personally fulfilled, to sing your song and to contribute to the success of others. You have learned that social media is about 'collecting and sharing knowledge' and social networks are about 'collecting and sharing people'.

I may have challenged your thoughts by asking you to be open, random and supportive and to rid yourself of any of your old values of being closed, selective and controlling. There are some amazing people in this new world; connecting with them across the wealth of social media and social networks will change your life.

The movement that you can become part of is far greater than any of us can actually see. We are the pioneers. It is going to be the most amazing change in the history of the modern world. The beginning of the Individual Revolution, moving from 150 years of the Industrial Revolution when companies, not individuals, held the power.

Finally, my dream is that we stop seeing these networks as e-commerce, sales engines or as media marketing machines. Instead we should see these networks as humanity networks, full of people that are part of the change we all want. Together we are making this change. With your input the world can become more connected, working as one to increase global wealth and reduce friction and anger.

When we are part of this movement we can feel it in our fingertips. As we immerse ourselves through our keyboards into the networks we can sense the emotion. This is not technology, it is the people inside these networks that are truly incredible, the people who share unconditionally and in doing so become the most respected and attractive people in their industries.

I am driven by this change. Social media gives you your voice, it provides the environment and the philosophy for you to create change in your life and while doing this you can help others to achieve their dreams.

Enjoy this new world and watch your personal, emotional and spiritual wealth build in ways you previously thought impossible. It is not just financial wealth that you will achieve, the rewards are far greater than that.

Thank you for reading this book. I hope this has helped you to create clarity and generate enthusiasm towards this very exciting new world.

If you would like to join the community of people who have read this book and believe in the philosophy that I have shared please visit my blog at www.knowmelikemefollowme.com

You can also follow me on Twitter @knowlikefollow and observe the conversation on Twitter #knowme.

SOURCES OF INFORMATION

1 http://www.statistics.gov.uk/pdfdir/lmsuk1008.pdf
2 http://www.sethgodin.com/permission/
3 http://en.wikipedia.org/wiki/Maslow%27s_hierarchy_of_
  needs
4 http://southasia.oneworld.net/todaysheadlines/ilo-
  predicts-global-unemployment-growth-by-20-million
5 http://www.pru.co.uk/retireourway/getthefacts/changing_
  retirement_landscape/living_longer/
6 http://www.imrg.org/8025741F0065E9B8/(httpNews)/
  924F4DDD502BD014802574FD00354FB8?Open
  Document
7 http://www.childrensociety.org.uk/resources/documents/
  good%20childhood/Executive%20summary%20of%20
  launch%20report_2723_full.pdf
8 http://borndigitalbook.com/about.php
9 http://en.wikipedia.org/wiki/Self-esteem
10 Tapscott, D. (2006) *Wikinomics*, Portfolio Publishing
11 Leboff, Grant (2007) *Sales Therapy*, Capstone Publishing
12 http://www.ecademy.com/account.php?id=183254

13 http://www.ecademy.com/node.php?id=122547

14 http://www.ecademy.com/account.php?id=312261

15 http://www.ecademy.com/account.php?id=78336

16 http://www.youtube.com/watch?v=D1R-jKKp3NA

17 http://parkeladd.com/2009/26/the-dip-seth-godin/

18 Earls, Mark (2007) *Herd: How to Change Mass Behaviour by Harnessing Our True Nature*, John Wiley & Sons

19 http://www.ecademy.com/node.php?id=122547&cid=59 3286&pid=0#593286

20 http://www.ecademy.com/account.php?id=308551

21 http://www.happyandprosperous.com/about/

22 http://www.happyand prosperous.com/2007/12/03/drains-and-radiators/

23 http://www.bni.com/Default.aspx?tabid=626

24 http://www.ecademy.com/node.php?id=10572

25 http://www.rogerhamilton.com/

26 http://xlgroupblog.com/vision-2020

27 http://en.wikipedia.org/wiki/Hermann_Hesse

28 http://www.ecademy.com/account.php?id=162229 (Let Go section)

29 http://en.wikipedia.org/wiki/Mantra

30 http://www.charlieplumb.com/

31 http://www.ecademy.com/node.php?id=102349

32 Friedman, Thomas L. (2008) *Hot, Flat and Crowded*, Farrar, Straus and Giroux

33 http://www.ecademy.com/account.php?id=37979

34 http://www.nigelrisner.com/

35 http://www.ecademy.com/account.php?id=42441

36 http://www.ecademy.com/node.php?id=58291

37 http://en.wikipedia.org/wiki/Carl_Jung

38 www.potential-unlimited.com

39 http://en.wikipedia.org/wiki/Chris_Anderson_(writer)

40 http://www.thelongtail.com/

41 http://en.wikipedia.org/wiki/Fred_Wilson_(financier)

42 http://www.wired.com/

43 http://www.techdirt.com/articles/20070503/012939.shtml

44 http://www.ecademy.com/node.php?id=112250

45 http://www.ecademy.com/node.php?id=112249

46 http://www.ecademy.com/account.php?=427943

47 http://www.ecademy.com/account.php?id=92889

48 http://www.ecademy.com/node.php?id=117956

49 http://www.ecademy.com/account.php?id=264578

50 http://www.ecademy.com/account.php?id=72197

51 http://www.mercuri.net/site/global

52 http://wordpress.org/

53 http://www.blogger.com/start

54 http://www.ecademy.com/account.php?id=64085

55 http://www.ecademy.com/account.php?id=128575

56 http://www.ecademy.com/account.php?id=42737

57 http://www.ecademy.com/account.php?id=37979

58 http://www.icarusconsultants.com/about_us

59 http://www.ecademy.com/account.php?id=265107

60 http://www.winningbysharing.net/aboutauthor.asp

61 http://en.wikipedia.org/wiki/Servant_leadership

62 http://twitter.com/dirkthecow

63 http://www.ecademy.com/account.php?id=235339

64 http://www.ecademy.com/account.php?id=53930

INDEX

Note: Page numbers in bold indicate major treatments.